MW01658135

Porcupine literary arts magazine

Volume 8
Issue 1

Cover Art

Cover: *Water Lilies,* 45" x 45"
Oil on aluminum, 2003 by Mai Wyn Schantz

Back Cover: *Stuckey Bay,* 36" x 30"
Oil on aluminum, 2003 by Mai Wyn Schantz

Acknowledgements

Porcupine Literary Arts Magazine is supported, in part, by a grant from the Wisconsin Arts Board with funds from the State of Wisconsin, and by the Kohler Foundation.

We also thank these individuals, without whom publication of this issue would not have been possible:

Charlotte & Jere Richardson   Diana Avery

Porcupine is a not for profit literary arts magazine published semiannually in Cedarburg, Wisconsin 53012 (P.O. Box 259).

Phone: 262-375-3128 email: Ppine259@aol.com
Website: http://members.aol.com/ppine259

There is no distinct edge between art forms, between the artists' works and lives, between one artist's work and another's. Artists connect people to each other, people to the earth, the present to the past and future.

Visual art work and poetry, short fiction and other literary manuscripts will be given prompt attention, but must be accompanied by a self-addressed, stamped envelope. One-time publishing rights have been granted to Porcupine. All copyrights are retained by the authors.

Porcupine is produced on a Macintosh® computer system using QuarkXpress™.
The text is set in 10 pt. Sabon Roman and Italic, with headlines and captions in Sabon and various weights and styles of Formata.

ISSN: 1547-8548

Indexed by *The American Humanities Index*

International Standard Book Number: 0-9752710-0-8

Table of Contents

Lauro Palomba

Fiction

The Scoop On Our Rob

The drill bakes your brain, overcooks your legs into soggy noodles and boils your blood like chili sauce. It goes like this.

You rush in from the baseline. From across the net, beside a buggy swarming with yellow balls, the instructor swats one of the furry things at you. You volley the ball to either side of him and keep charging till you reach the net. You slap it with your racquet and then immediately get on your horse and back-pedal like mad because the instructor has lofted a lob that sends you practically back to the baseline. You lift your left arm for balance, as you've been shown, draw a bead on the descending blob and whack an overhead smash into the instructor's court. You refocus on him and already here comes ball two for you to volley.

And three. And four. And five.

The instructor's pushing for ten but by the sixth repetition you're woozy and you can't latch on to a breath. With your ebbing strength you squeal, "Next!" and wobble off the court to await renewed punishment.

For our Rob, this gruelling drill was only the half of it; he also had to worry how he looked while running his guts out. This was not, you understand, a guy with a gimpy ego. But he moved like a gazelle and he was zoned, as the pros say, a laser concentration. I don't think Lili noticed that a fair number of his volleys high jumped the fence or that some overheads damn near vamoosed over the clouds.

But when he sidled off, after seven, squawking "Next!" in a ragged pant, chest throbbing and verve shot, conserving enough of his wits to wink at her, she was all eyes.

Robert David Michael had three Christian names and no obvious surname so that, as he aged, no one would be sure where to preface the 'Mr.' and thereby tip him off to his own mortality.

That would be my lead if I were doing a profile of him. Naturally, a word-withering, tabloid editor would compress it to something like: Robert Michael thought he'd buck the trend. Or maybe: Time takes no prisoners.

When I think of Rob, I recall something Anais Nin said of Henry Miller's wife, June: Her beauty brings drama and events to her. It's true. People can't leave beauty alone. They don't make googoo eyes from afar. They want to get in close and commandeer it. That makes for adventure.

Already Rob was casual about his fame. After all, hadn't he been on French TV last summer, playing guitar outside Les Invalides and being interviewed in the company of other slumming youth whose non-conformity was subsidized by their conformist parents? The young have so much youth they squander it. If those are the sour grapes of an over-thirty, it's because I am.

Now the poets would have you believe that beauty goes with truth or purity, a cloudless night or a nice cheese sauce. Mainly, beauty goes with itself; it has masturbatory qualities. It's its own reward. Or, alas, it hogs another beauty– like love-crossed movie stars– and leaves the rest of us disconsolate.

But it's saddening to witness God's perversity. He creates such perfection, then unmuzzles the years to maul His own creation. I say this because our Rob had come into possession of the whole kit: flashy height and athletically slim, with a simply beautiful head, sculpted muscles and bones, and burnished hair that washed up in your eyes more glamorously than Cote D'Azur waves at sunset.

I often imagined his cherub soul peering into the water at poolside, heartsmitten at the reflection, while he pleaded through his sonorous pipes to God for more. God, lighting a tycoon cigar as he rolled it in the O of His mouth, indulged the latest request, puffed on His omnipotence and, overlooking the dollops of charm He'd already implanted, replied, "Oh hell, give it to him!"

Early on, vanity had leaked into Rob's soul and God left that in too.

In short, the sweet talker who couldn't last two drafts of beer– usually paid with my money– without whetting the barmaid had everything but substance. Still, he gave off a life force at ease with the college pub we usually drank in: bay windows of spring sunshine, plants of potted health, wood-warm tables and chairs in a spaciousness opening onto a patio where chunky hamburgers were barbecued for sale.

To be honest, I've slightly overdrawn him. Defects he had. The skin under his chin could've been tighter. He was a stripling twenty-three but, unless altered by a cosmetic surgeon, our Rob had a head start on jowliness. With his debauches weighing it lower, a middle-age flap was in the works.

Incredulity at his windfall hurt him too. He couldn't believe his surplus blessings and needed to enhance them. Here's what I mean. At a friend's house one evening, to attract attention, Ezra Pound grabbed the red tulips decorating the dinner table and began to eat them. Well, Rob would've drunk the vase water to boot.

When the outrageous gesture was limited by his imagination or indifference, Rob passed out showy remarks like a salesman passes out his business cards. These remarks were all free association without an umbilical cord tying them to anything vital, and intended only as scoring points; the way Olympic fencers lunge and jab without consequence.

An example. We'd be in the pub having a skull session on religion, the decline of spirituality, and Rob would toss this off: "Jesus spoke in parables. If He'd been Spanish, He'd have spoken in palabras." Probably because of my advertising background, I prized cleverness and Rob would hook me with his twaddle.

However, it didn't blind me to his faults. So it wasn't a comedown for me when stories circulated that Rob had cheated on his Christmas take-home economics exam by consulting the family banker. The economics prof wanted him expelled for plagiarism but the journalism dean refused to run him out unless a supporting source came forward. Now tell me, who's going to incriminate himself for abetting fraud and injure beauty in the same breath?

Meanwhile, Candice, his girlfriend and actress in our serial male fantasies, was writing most of his major essay. When you're photogenic with a smooth patter and you speak in insights, you shouldn't have to do the lowly groundwork required for the degree. Besides, Rob already had a summer job lined up at a TV station out west. This foot in the door would inevitably make him master of the house. That was his prediction. Buy Rob four beers and he'd play an anchor simulating a daffy newscast. With the future mapped, studying towards a journalism degree was a filler, a dry run on camera angles, on polishing his charisma and refining his journalistic techniques. An advertisement for himself.

I'll own up that we weren't tight buddies during the course. What we had in common was the role of outsiders to the weekend partying gangs. Because I was older, because my concerns weren't theirs, I detoured around the temptations; Rob, on the other hand, was always booked from Friday to Sunday for more personalized high jinks and simply unavailable.

Maybe at this point, in the interests of that myth of journalistic objectivity, I should present my credentials before continuing.

Journalism, which hadn't attracted me the first time around university, became a desirable second chance. After my first tour of academic life, I'd consecrated myself to poetry. Sensible isn't my middle name. It took five years to admit my poems would never ripple the literary pond but once words have affected your brain, you're never cured. So admitting my failure was no antibiotic at all.

I was sick with rhythms and quatrains. All the time I was in advertising, the six years of fraying marriage, raising our sons, the sickness ate me up. When the quarrels came with Sandra, my wife– over money, boredom, relocation, the leather couch, a painting that wasn't even an original, and isn't it chintzy to fight over inanimate things?– I suspected it was really my failure getting in its last licks but we called it divorce.

My ex and I decided to redo ourselves. She opened a ceramics boutique with a potter and I returned to university to prepare for a living through journalism; words less potent and concentrated than poetry but creative nonetheless.

Since that had been my choice and I'd forsaken my salary and promotion– what the economics prof taught me was my opportunity cost for attending his course– I dedicated myself to doing well rather than skipping classes, sleeping in late, going through booze as through a car wash and luring bedmates. That and being the oldest in the class made me an odd bird.

Worse, my classmates had never heard of poetry. To them, Dylan Thomas could be the lead singer of a rock band. Or the rock band itself. I was friendly and tipsy at the college pub but avoided the gin and hashish binges at their apartments. Not that I had many offers. A suspected dirty old man is a lecher whereas a confirmed dirty young man is an appetizing rake. I was thirty-six and there was no mending that. Rob was loudly addressed in class by one of his early partners as Studly. I, without cause, was whispered to be of the soiled, over-the-hill variety though never openly labelled a predator of young flesh.

That said, here are the goods that I can vouch for on our

Rob. I noticed him on the first day as he was targeting Candice. We'd gathered in the lounge to have our pictures taken for the yearbook and his radar picked her immediately. As I was to learn, Candice had modelled in her teens and I figured she and Rob would be a match before long. Later, I concluded that she'd grown smarter through her beauty rather than simply milking it for a series of passing larks.

Rob was something else. Two months into our graduate program, nearly every woman he craved in the class, even those who saw through him, had been sucked in and spat out to dry in the afternoon glare of his ego. The rest of us who hadn't been hoodwinked by his good looks– the envious males who hadn't become disciples, the unsought females, and the two or three who were still resisting– seldom saw him quiet or alone. Even if something had moved us to seek a connection with him, we wouldn't have known where to attach our affection.

When the twelve-month graduate program began in the late spring, we were assigned an office together on the second floor of the college's turret tower. That wasn't much of an icebreaker because neither of us was ever there. I'd sit occasionally in that claustrophobic room to escape my hyperkinetic classmates and their homework story ideas. From my alcove, if the wind was right, I'd listen to the thwack of tennis balls from the nearby courts. A fairy tale of trees blocked the window's view and those thwacks seemed to come from a magical kingdom. From the spacing of the thwacks and the shouts, I'd try to visualize the game in progress and the skill level of the players. When the courts were waterlogged after a tempest, I'd watch hares, chipmunks and squirrels hopping into the underbrush.

About three months in, during the sessions devoted to writing a lead, Rob and I began finding each other shipwrecked in the pub. While the others were on their fifth draft of converting their undergraduate essay-opening paragraphs into twenty-word tabloid eye catchers, Rob and I drank in the first floor pub. I'd finished quickly because of my advertising experience. He didn't give a damn what he wrote; his future lay in television.

It was one of the few courses underway during the summer and the campus was a serenely empty and restful place. Rob and I discovered we liked beer and tennis and confined our meetings to those occasions.

The first morning we arranged to play he was forty minutes late. Of course, he was a serve and volleyer; no drama in playing from the baseline. Every time he came to net and lost the point, he'd boast his complaint of being tired because some blonde, Candice maybe, had kept him up all night. The more excuses he made for his shoddy play, the more I enjoyed whizzing passing shots by him, sometimes hammering one at his hip. He was a tad slow– I guess he'd left the drive in his legs on the blonde's mattress– and often out of position. Spitefully, I'd lob him now and again to really see him in pain.

Then, by summer's end, when I'd cuckolded the stud, the secret gave me an edge. Whenever I was temporarily behind in our match, it made me smug and I'd put some extra oomph into my forehands.

In the animal world, the aggressive and colourful male is often dominant. But anthropologists say that in some ape species, the female monkey mates not just with the chest-thumpers but also– on the sly– with the shy, weaker ones. One Friday night, he and Candice had had a tiff or he'd gone poaching elsewhere unannounced. It was term's end and she'd been typing his essay before finishing her own. It put the three of us on deadline to meet our degree requirements, rare among the class of forty-one. It was more her sorrow than any consolation I might offer but she came home with me.

I was renting a house where in the daytime robins ran across the sunlit back lawn like late commuters and the neighbour's calico cat stalked them in vain. It was already sprinkling when we got in. The bedroom's glass doors led directly into the yard and by the time we'd shunted into that room the outdoors were very elemental. The place had atmosphere. Thunder, lightning, all these magnificent noises. The house had no eavestroughs and the rain cascaded straight down from the roof, splashing into its own carved ditch. With the doors open, the curtains tied at the edges and just the screen in place, I couldn't tell looking past her storm-whipped head whether it was her or the trees moaning in the dark. My only fear was of an intruder appearing– maybe the neighbour searching for his depressed cat– and scaring the hell out of us.

Afterwards she stood by the screen, seemingly triggering at will the lightning flashes retreating to the east. I had a yen to slide open the screen door and step out with her onto the aroused, sopping lawn, to touch the danger of a balmy July night, she flitting naked like a robin and me the cat.

Sex is never about just getting laid. Never. I remember the session making me feel unseasoned and simple again, as I hadn't felt since before my marriage. When lovers in their twenties get it on, it's mazy but robust. Years later, the partners are lugging so many bygone lovers onto the bed for each bout, it's attitude rather than action.

"I'd like him to see me now," she said in silhouette.

"Would it bother him?"

"I doubt it."

I knew it was a one-shot affair with her and didn't mind having been of service. "Then you've made a mistake."

She looked over her shoulder and I wished a flash of light would reveal the smile I hoped was there. "No, it was nice. Different." After my break-up with Sandra, I'd developed the unreasonable fear that the next lovemaking might be my last and maybe my gratefulness had come through. "You're older. You're used to things taking their time. You think telling him would smarten him up?"

"Can't say. I just know his tennis. Take a chance. You a gambler?"

"Not really."

"I think people should gamble." I said it with a false authority meant to distract and cheer her.

"And have him blow his stack?"

"Do it to find out if you're lucky. You could be walking around lucky and not know it."

"Was your degree in psychology?"

"English. Major in doggerel."

"Then you can't explain it."

"Explain what?"

"He closes his eyes when he comes and he leaves me. He goes off on his own, behind his eyes. Like it's all his doing."

"So why do you stick around?"

"He says I'm a sure thing. Isn't that what we're all looking for? Someone good, someone straight? But it's like he's throwing it in my face."

It didn't seem so odd to me. A wayward guy, a wayward drift. My working life had knocked the stars out of my romantic heavens and I tried to pass on the favour. "We were preparing for an ad on a hygiene product once and we came across this study on orgasms. Seems that when women have an orgasm there's a change in air pressure in the uterus. Before orgasm, the air pressure is positive. Then it reverses and that creates suction. This draws in sperm and increases your chance of getting pregnant. The researcher said it was a form of mate choice. It lets the woman control who fertilizes her eggs."

"If she can control herself."

"Well, that's the catch."

"It would be."

We stayed friendly after that night. Whenever she looked to be in the dumps, I'd pick up her spirits in the corridor by asking, "How's that air pressure?" Rob kept tampering with it throughout the winter, from what I learned second-hand after the snows came and the tennis stopped. I didn't see much of either of them. In the final term, I specialized in print and they signed up for electronic journalism. I practised reporting and layout on the school newspaper and they were frequently absent, busily shooting and editing videotape, making and splicing audio recordings and simulating newscasts in the studio.

Our trip to the instructional tennis camp in North Carolina took root in April. I was in the pub brightening a ridiculously late snowfall through the sunny filter of a large glass of brew. We'd just written the law course final exam.

"What a bitch," Rob said, plopping beside me and– wonder of wonders– pushing across a bottle he'd paid for to top up my diminishing suds.

"Did you finish?"

"Too tired. More thinking than I've done all year."

"You think you muffed it?"

"So what? Media organizations have lawyers to vet everything that goes on air. Their bag is libel, mine is a good story."

"How's the major essay coming?"

"Didn't you hear? The dean's extended the date to September."

"Love those hard deadlines," I said.

"You're just pissed because you finished yours in February. Serves you right for being a keener. How you gonna kill these last two weeks?"

"I was thinking of hanging out at a tennis camp down south. Humble myself one last time before launching my illustrious second career. Catch a few rays, work on the strokes, straighten out some bad habits."

"Oh yeah? Doesn't sound half bad. Here it's all over but the formalities. You driving down alone? I think I come across the screen better with a tan."

And so off we went. We bypassed the interstate and did some sightseeing on the back roads of Pennsylvania. By nightfall, we were dizzy with mountain turns. After chowing at a chicken joint, he bought a bottle of Southern Comfort– ambiance, he called it, for our introduction to the American South– and got sloshed in the motel room. We watched a hockey playoff game for a while and I tried to lure him into an account of his affair with Candice. I suppose my interviewing technique needed polishing because by game's end he was babbling about his mother instead.

He had a pillow propped on the headboard and sprawled on the blanket in his underwear and t-shirt. What a fine physique it was, ideal for draping in the chicest duds. He'd be a natural for assignments to the entertainment scene. The Southern Comfort in his hand he warmed in the cove of his groin. Occasionally, he thrust it over to me for a snort.

I lowered the volume on the TV set and in the same movement pressed 'record' on my tape recorder lying on the night stand between our beds. This is a snippet of what I caught, the rest being mush.

"My mama doesn't like poetry. And she doesn't fancy fiction. It ends in disarray... and that array. No conclusion. She hates it that those damn characters can go on. My mama laps up biographies. Know why? The person dies and guarantees her a good cry. I was doing homework in the living room one night. She was reading the final chapters and when she shut this huge mother on Richard Burton, the African explorer not the actor, her eyes were wet. Out of the blue she says to me, 'This is your time, Robbie. Billions before you have had theirs. Some died in foreign places looking for adventure or on a personal mission. Some died at home playing it safe. Most of them never gave their time a thought. And this is yours. You'll join them soon enough. But for now, it's your time. It's more than they can say.'"

He took an extended swig from the bottle. "She reads

and nibbles on Swiss cheese and pita bread and the tears run into her mouth while she's chewing. Because she knows the ending. Everybody's ending is the same. That ain't no late breaking news. But I don't wanna have the endings plotted in advance. Jeez, I hate biographies."

His throatiness gave the impression that what had passed through his pipes had been clouded by more than hooch, had gone misty with unexpected confession. And I thought, where'd this twitch come from? It wouldn't be an emotion, would it?

The tape has me asking– which I don't recall– "How can you hate biographies? I thought an apple never falls far from the tree?"

Our Rob, back to his old self, answers, "My mother planted on a slope."

It was as close as I'd heard him come to soul searching; whether in his soul or for his soul being another matter. By noon the next day he'd sobered up but he did make another slip early in the morning. We were passing a locked church that was preaching all the same. On a sign on its lawn, under the pastor's name and the hours of service, was this cautionary bulletin for travellers: Smooth sailing doesn't make experienced sailors.

"That's what I was talking about," Rob mumbled, munching on a chunk from his doughnut and trying to sip his coffee without staining my upholstery.

That evening at a motel and gasoline strip in Sutton, West Virginia, he trotted out the familiar Rob. The sassy, mandolin-hipped waitress came to clear our salad dishes at the seafood buffet restaurant; her first mistake was friendliness.

"Are y'all from around here?" The way her eyes fawned on him, she hoped he was.

He turned his high beams on her. "No, are you?"

"Yeah. But I left home when I was thirteen." She implied she'd run off and been independent since then. "I went to Oklahoma. I was alone. They'd as soon stab you there as say hello. I came back."

"Where were you born in West Virginia?" I asked. She was a knockout and I wanted to bathe in her radiance a little longer.

"Right over there. The other side of the ridge."

"What's on the other side?" Rob asked, teasing a secret from his shy admirer.

She smiled. "Heaven."

It might have been a town or a feeling. "I wish I had someone to show it to me," he said, his wattage outshining hers.

When it's in abundance, I tend to attack food like a famished farmer and not speak civilly. I don't relent until the food gives up. He was way ahead of me anyway. Waiting in line to get a second crack at the shrimp, I could see Rob rubbing his heating lotion deep into her hormones. By the time she scooped up our dessert plates, I'd pigged out and he had a rendezvous.

At midnight, I went for a walk, partly to help digestion, maybe to catch them nearby, but traffic on the interstate had slowed and the service road into town was deserted. It was cool with only the crickets working hard and the moon playing coy behind some rising fog and moody black jigsaw clouds. In the parking lot outside the restaurant about to close, the sliding door had fallen off a van and the parents were bickering while the kids toyed with their boredom.

I was sleeping when he came in. I heard him in the shower around nine the next morning and when I yawned and asked how it had gone, he replied, "Heaven." Which seemed unnecessarily restrained coming from him.

We cruised as far as Fort Lauderdale-by-the-sea to check out any hardbodies on the beach. What we saw was one seagull holding off five while protecting and picking at a pizza slice discarded on the street. A felon gale mugged us for three days. The palm trees bowed in servitude and the rip currents had the ocean to themselves. Gray, white-headed pelicans had hunkered down beside the pier. With their heads sunk into their windblasted feathers, they looked like curling stones. Our most exotic encounter occurred with five Brazilians who hardly spoke English, weren't sure of the direction to Disney World, couldn't remove the gas cap from their rental van and were helpless in operating the self-serve pumps. The day it stubbornly rained, we queued through an Annie Leibowitz exhibition at the Museum of Art.

The sun came out to see us off. A model was posing for a photographer on the median of Las Olas Boulevard. Rob insisted on watching the shoot. We followed them to the hotel where the session continued with the lady busting wetly out of her bikini in the outdoor, kidney-shaped pool with the inland waterway as background. No surprise when Rob got out his video camera and began filming her too, which ticked off the photographer to no end. His warnings to Rob and Rob's waving them off aggravated into a shoving match. I nearly took one in the chops while separating them but Rob still managed to dangle a few propositions to the model before the photographer hustled her away. So Rob, hoping her room was booked on the street side, tried an endgame of roller-skating backwards outside the hotel using his cut-off top as a billowing sail to show off his tight tummy. But nothing came of it.

We moseyed on to Savannah, Georgia. It was the Thursday before Good Friday, hot and quiet, probably the same as it had dawned on Golgotha before the carpenters arrived. We'd been walking through the antebellum neighbourhoods and when I saw Rob's curiosity about to raise the white flag, I took his video camera and posed him in front of a corner house. The guidebook said it was constructed in the 1850s but it wasn't a carriage house like most of the others. The three-story brick building had a chest-high wall which created a small courtyard and blocked out pedestrians. A brown wooden gate, arched at its top, swung out from the wall where ivy bearded its street face.

A fortyish woman in a grey sweatshirt with similar colour streaking her untinted hair, walked out the gate behind him with a potted plant in her hand. She braked, apologized and scampered aside to wait on the road while I videoed Rob. We exchanged some pleasantries, informed her of our backgrounds and destination. Her questions seemed genuine like she'd been a frequent traveller herself.

Rob asked rather thoughtfully, not in the interview style I'd been using, "Is this a lifelong dream come true?"

"Actually, it's our first house," she said warmly, maybe startled by such a dead-on question coming from this strapping lad. "We're from Manhattan. My husband and I, our families don't have much history and we've always wanted to own something like this."

"I heard the only green thumbs in Manhattan got that way from counting money," he pressed her.

"I grew up in Connecticut. My father kept a garden."

"You find yourself keeping the curtains closed because of the tourists taking pictures?" This from a guy wanting to succeed in television land where he'd have to poke his lense behind thick facades and under thin skins.

"Oh no, it's the jasmine they keep picking."

I asked her some follow-up questions and when I looked around, I saw Rob up the street under a tree overhung with Spanish moss as though a tub of boiled spinach had exploded over its branches. I thought he'd acted like a dog that, having gotten the bone it wanted, goes off to savour it in solitude. But walking up to rejoin him, admiring that spinach-like cascade above his head, it flashed to me that he and the moss weren't that foreign to each other. The guidebook said Spanish moss was an epiphytic, a plant that grows on another but isn't parasitic, and I wondered if his brief exchange with the woman hadn't shown him capable of belonging to such a species.

Since we were running ahead of schedule, we detoured to Charleston, South Carolina. It had a sunny prettiness but what I remember was a doorway with a broken step leading down a dim corridor of deteriorating orange plaster and a warping tile floor with a black and white diamond design. At the entrance, a small white sign screwed above the address warned: Attention. Chat Lunatique.

The next day we curved into Asheville, racquets unsheathed and itching to do harm to those little yellow balls. We were spoiling for combat.

The Blue Ridge Tennis School in Thomas Wolfe's hometown snuggled in one of the folds of an 18-hole golf course which itself formed part of the grounds of a resort and conference center. The four outdoor tennis courts were swathed by the rolling topography of the Blue Ridge Mountains. I wasn't a golfer but the wavy fairways made me feel for the hacker who missed the flat greens on the approach. Picking up speed as it fell away, the ball could roll till Wolfe's resurrection and you'd be pitching back up from Georgia.

It was lovely and distracting to have the courts in the scooped out hollow beneath the hotel. During our pauses, we'd watch the duffers struggling at their game as we were at ours. All the cloudless days, stray golf shots cut through the surrounding branches sounding like nuts falling in the autumn woods. The accountant from Atlanta, too lazy to walk down from the hotel, ignored the posted notices and took a dinger on the rear door of his red Mercedes that he'd parked in the lot. He hunted down and pocketed the offending ball, lying to the player who soon turned up to retrieve it.

We were a baker's dozen, though one dropped out after the first day, and a friendly batch at that. Our advanced group consisted of myself, the spiteful accountant and a bubbly couple from Virginia who were colour-matched daily– teal one day, black tops and pink shorts the next. It was the fourth time they'd taken the course and their picture hung in the office alongside those of other sunburnt customers. When the husband confided that he dealt with a great deal of tension in his job, Rob suggested, just brimming with sympathy, "Have you thought of having your tension re-strung?"

Rob belonged in our level but he had mysteriously regressed. Typically, he popped up beside Lili on Monday morning as we clustered to begin our stretching and warm-up exercises. The real jolt lay in my right-handed companion having become a southpaw overnight. When the tennis pro ran us through some simple groundstrokes to determine our ability, Rob, having watched Lili spray balls into the adjoining court, stepped forward with the racquet in his left hand and, in a display of natural awkwardness, earned himself a spot in the novice category with her.

Lili was in her mid-twenties, blonde, green-eyed, with bosomy and kissable lips. She was peppy but rooted it in an inner steadiness. I liked her in traditional white, her ponytail wagging through the hole in her cap. She moved to the ball with respect. I'd seen the bimbo flirts who showed up in high heels to impress the tennis pro with their toned legs. Lili and her friend Lisa were vacationing from the northwest near where Rob planned to initiate his career.

Lisa was easy on the eyes and a shade taller than me but otherwise unremarkable. She fit into the intermediate squad and I was free to concentrate on the exacting tennis which left me sore, bushed and wonderfully sated. The groups would rotate through the instructors on the staggered courts and sometimes we and the novices would practise side-by-side on the lower courts. Then I had a chance to study Rob worming into Lili's heart: offering Lili praise and support, making her laugh at her mistakes, caressing her elbow as he helped her with her serve.

The four of us had rum and cokes in the hotel lounge late one afternoon. Lili had an intelligence fine as her figure– Rob's tastes were damn near infallible– and Lisa was pleasant enough but I might as well have made the trip alone. Lisa had an aunt in the area and after the lessons I'd tour Asheville on my own and eat in some chain restaurant or other. Pretty soon, I had our room to myself as Rob stopped coming back at night. I didn't really mind. The five hours of tennis drained me and I preferred my evenings quiet.

On Thursday, the second-last night, the school had planned sandwiches and Greek salad outdoors with the instructors. Lisa arrived by herself. I hadn't expected the lovebirds to waste their precious moments on tuna and ham and cheese. She filled her plate and came to the picnic table where I was waiting for my Virginia teammates.

"They've left, you know."

"Who?"

"Lili and Rob."

"Left what?"

"The hotel, the tennis. In her car."

I'd seen something coming though not at that speed. It didn't make sense. Why entangle himself with Lili when there were more treasures to raid? "How are you getting home?"

"I was hoping you could give me a lift north and then I'll take a plane."

"No problem." It would be my contribution to their runaway infatuation. What a jerk. Just up and leave. No explanation or apology required for the chauffeur, me. The bastard. His manners were in his balls. "It'll be nice to drive back with someone else. We were spending too much time together anyway," I mocked, but she missed it.

So there they were, gonadal and loose on the highway, Lili's excitement wide as the lanes. Of course she'd want to learn all about him. Ask and you shall be deceived. It was a pun we used on an advertising campaign.

"Maybe they'll live happily ever after."

A cheesy strand clotheslined out from Lisa's mouth; her finger hooked and plucked it like a harp. "I hope so," she replied, "because ever after may be pretty short."

Oh? Had our boy outfoxed himself? A little comeuppance? He kick-started his feelings with these transitory intrigues but now he'd picked up someone even more adept at shedding partners. It looked good on him.

"She's one of these love 'em and leave 'em types, is she?"

"It's her health. She's not well."

"What does she have?" An early onset of varicose veins to spoil his enjoyment of her legs? It was a distasteful tack for me because to nail him I had to wish ill of her.

"Amyotrophic lateral sclerosis."

I stared for a second, checking her face for exaggeration. "Seriously?"

"It's degenerative. It destroys your body functions. That's why she wanted to learn tennis before it became obvious."

Unforgiving and nasty, I said, "She's more unlucky than she thinks. Rob's a carefree bird. All things bright and beautiful and that stuff. I can't see him in a hospital ward."

Even if the weasel had a wisp of compassion, he'd pervert the moment with his grandstanding. I doubted he'd be capable of seeing it through to the end of her suffering. He wasn't about to take up celibate sainthood. I remembered something by a saint, St. Jerome I think: pain falls on the heart, drop by drop, and turns to wisdom. That would really be going over the top for Rob. But even if he stuck it out, I pictured this scene: Lili, emaciated, brave, sinking; Rob holding her limp hand. Before she drew the final breath that pulled down her eyelids, our Rob the showman would lean towards her and whisper. Whisper something stagy like "I'll see you on the other side. You bring the tennis balls." Whisper, but within earshot of the family and relatives gathered at the bedside, and with tenderness, a tiny bit of which he'd acquired for the purpose.

I didn't want to pursue my resentment any further or

emphasize to Lisa the likelihood of Rob being long gone before her friend got around to revealing her tragedy. So I speculated aloud: "He'll be in for a shock when he finds out."

All the while she couldn't speak because of her mouthful, she was shaking her head. Then reaching for her drink, she said, "He knows. She told him. Just before he asked her to go away."

Lauro Palomba is a civilian teaching English as a Foreign Language to Asian and Eastern and Central European military officers and diplomats at a military base north of Toronto, Ontario. Work has been published or is forthcoming in more than a dozen literary journals.

Karyna McGlynn

Poetry

Non-Traditional Student

Sounds a little too correct, sensitive,
quick wash over my age which, after all,
could be anything over twenty-one.

I sip coffee with slight astringency,
shame in falling, splat, outside the ranks
of normal matriculation, body huge
and thrust up through the turf, red and naked
mole-rat heaving across the spider-veins
of campus pathway. I sit cross-legged
and uncomfortable on the quad's jade coif.

Students charge expensive bread
on their dorm keys. Gardeners go about
their work, careful not to look
girls in the eye or up and down.
The fountain just goes and goes
in the deep blue cling of late September.

I forgot this abundance, this deep net,
life's entrance modeled on Eden,
and everywhere, archways leading in
and through and out if you trip up,
if they notice your eyes crinkle a bit
at the corners in unorthodox knowledge,

that the voice lacks a certain tang
of well-masked fear, of girls trembling
with a first romantic freedom, skin standing
up from the bone in traditional vigil
through this, their sweetest season.

Karyna McGlynn is a writer and photographer living in Seattle. Her work recently appeared or is forthcoming in *Wisconsin Review, Poetry Salzburg Review, Plainsongs, The Blue Mouse*, and others. She is the editor of Screaming Emerson Press, which publishes chapbooks by local spoken-word poets.

Mekeel McBride

Poetry

Egg, Oracle, Brooch, Sunflower Petal, Hors D'Oeurve and Sailboat All Packed Safely in the Good Old Glowing Portmanteau

for Michael DePorte

And I turn and there's this moon, exactly the one
Chicky says you can't write about anymore
because it's been done, and it's old and nobody
cares. But it's my morning and this moon, full
and eggy, edges out of its sunrise nest singing,
I am not the Hunter's moon

because even something that far away knows
how sad I used to be with Abram Yosef Jack
who kept seven rifles under our bed, dead
and gutted deer hamstrung in the trees. And I
was one. I'm pretty sure this is something else
Chicky wouldn't like,

me saying the moon sang. But in its own way,
it did. And after *No longer Hunter's* I heard a pearl
turn into a word — *whole* — in parting
which made me so light-headed, I slipped
for awhile out of time to drift as it drifted
silently over the waking world like a great mother

of pearl platter, and it was leaving, all right, summer
shot to hell, too, with nothing to show for itself
but the trees falling to pieces. And a big sunflower
so burdened by the weight of its own life, its heavy head
lay flat against the earth, but in the end,
or so it seemed to me, only doubled over

in seed-heavy laughter. And Chicky can make
fun of the moon all he wants but he left a message,
once, on my machine, no words, just him, playing
the harmonica and if that music wasn't honeyed
with the kind of motion that lifts and fills
the white sail of the moon every night,

whether you can see it or not, then there is
no oxygen left on this earth but there's plenty,
of course, more than enough and that's the point,
isn't it, of a moon that floats like a glowing
suitcase down the night-into-sunrise river
of an ordinary October morning.

Travel

*

A pilgrim stops halfway across the bridge
to watch a padlocked chest drift down the river.
Whether it belongs to him or not
does not matter. What he needs, he carries
with him. It is not much. Soon he will be able
to set down even that small burden.

*

The room she kneels in is filled with light.
Dry grasses outside the window, tall and still.
One of her onyx hair combs has fallen,
black petal, onto the hardwood floor.
It is not her face she searches for as she gazes
into the shining water of the hand-held mirror.

Mekeel McBride teaches creative writing at the University of New Hampshire, and has five books of poetry with Carnegie Mellon University Press. He writes that his preferred job, however, is working at the Center for Wildlife in Cape Neddick, Maine, where he assists in wildlife rehabilitation. "It's not necessarily relevant, but my favorite animal is the porcupine. I have held a new baby in the palm of my hand, and driven an hour and a half to return a thirty pound adult (recovered from mange) to his home territory."

Taylor Graham

Poetry

Morning Hits Us

In the shed the goats clamor to come out
and gorge themselves on bear-clover,
that resiny forage they scorned last summer,
and dandle deer-brush like ice cream.

You called to say a friend can't stomach
food anymore, a side-effect of chemo.
Thank god, if I were to list my complaints
and failings, that wouldn't be one of them.

The goats know exactly what they want, this
mid-February day: virtue of the root pulsing
up from under what I thought of as winter.
I can't see anything pushing through soil

except the fragile shell-blue crocus.
How can anything so lovely heal us?

Bare Hands

My chores today are pulling weeds
and cataloguing Grandpa's books– the ones
he "liberated" from the Nazis. He can't remember,
any more, how his battalion climbed
the dragons' teeth to take Saarbrücken.
These days, he doesn't even notice
how his back yard's gone to crabgrass, snails,
dark thistle-dandelions growing fat and low
to the ground. It takes a long-handled hook
to hack and drag their roots out. Pale
green weeds like flowers spread from a tough,
kinky stem. I like how they snap out of soil
between my fingers. While I work, my dog
rolls in the clean, damp, weeded grass.

Grandpa's books are Sammelbilderbücher
left behind when the Hakenkreuz left town:
collectors' cards from cigarette packs:
in Der Weltkrieg, men and horses blown apart,
Amiens, Aug 1918. In the Kampf um's Dritte
Reich (1933), a chapter each for Göring
and Dr. Goebbels. Olympia 1936, the winter games
at Garmisch-Partenkirchen with pale
young heroes in racing gear and muscle.
Gramps doesn't remember how he brought them
from Saarbrücken by way of Dachau, home.

A Yugoslav lady who survived the camps
takes care of Grandpa now.
Looking out the window, she sees me
stooped to the dirt and she calls
out to ask, what filth
am I picking up with my bare
hands?

Taylor Graham is a volunteer search-and-rescue dog handler in the Sierra Nevada. Her poems have appeared in *Grand Street, The Iowa Review, The New York Quarterly, Poetry International,* and elsewhere. She's included in the new anthology, *California Poetry: Gold Rush to the Present* (Santa Clara University, 2004).

Featured Artist

Interview by W.A. Reed

Victoria Benson:
Diary of an Opera Singer

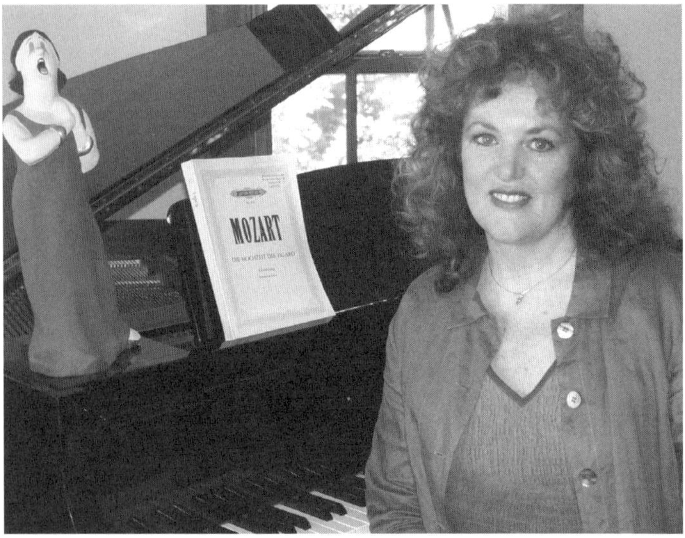

Photo by Vicki Reed

Victoria Benson left for Europe in the mid-eighties because she wanted a career in opera. She has since sung more than thirty leading roles in some six hundred performances and concerts in Germany, Austria, Switzerland, and most recently Wisconsin. Technically classified as an operetta diva, a direction she willingly took, European critics have praised her for her vocal beauty and flexibility, as well as for her interpretive flair. In addition to performing, Benson served as vocal coach for the Neumarkt Theatre and the Schauspiel Akademie, Zurich. She currently works with students from Marquette University, and apprentice artists of the Skylight Opera Company in Milwaukee, Wisconsin.

...Erich Seitter asked if I'd ever thought of doing operetta. The only music I had with me was <u>Somewhere Over the Rainbow</u> from <u>The Wizard of Oz</u>. So I sang that. He said I had a natural spark.

Porcupine: Operetta has been described by some as opera's giggly cousin.

Benson: In an opera, it's just singing, just music. In operetta, there are moments of dialogue– also, the traditions of a love-interest pair and the comic pair. The comic pair always has some number with a fun dance routine. That's the structural difference.

I found, as a performer, operetta roles to be much more challenging than those in opera. Because you have these very difficult songs to sing, the highs and lows of any opera, and then you have to break into dialogue– which I always did in German. In the opera roles, you have a chance to warm up throughout the performance. For the operetta diva, your entrance song would be one of the biggest pieces of the night.

Porcupine: And you have to step out there and just bang it out.

Benson: Exactly.

Porcupine: Are American show tunes considered an off-shoot of operetta?

Benson: It depends on which musicologist you talk to. I hesitate to compare the two, because operetta requires a trained voice and an opera sound. Therein lies the difference between the American musical comedy and operetta.

Porcupine: I've read that originally you were a mezzo

soprano whose future seemed to be in teaching, but that now you're a lyric soprano whose success has come from starring in German operas and operettas.

Benson: The difference, for me, is that I got with the right voice teacher and was able to open up the high notes. *Mezzo* comes from the Italian word that means *half*. That describes the voice that sings the lower roles. It's the lower female voice. The lyric soprano is a little higher, the one who sings the ballads. It's not the highest, where all the fireworks happen, just a little higher. In opera, the role of Carmen (Georges Bizet) is a mezzo. The role of Suzanna in the *The Marriage of Figaro* (Mozart) is a lyric soprano. Just to give you an idea of the differences.

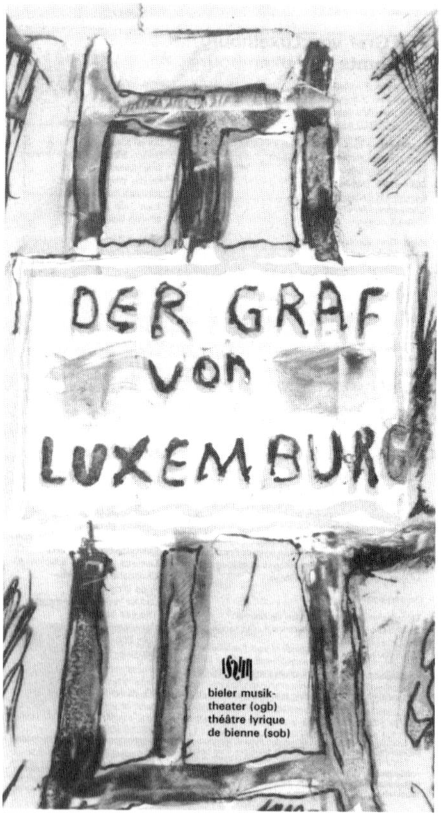

Translates– *The Count of Luxemburg*

"The first operetta I saw– when I didn't know what an operetta was. Ironically this was the last play I performed in before leaving Europe.

I had gone full circle."

–Victoria

Porcupine: Does a singer aspire to one or the other? Is one considered more the workhorse in opera?

Benson: Your voice type is determined by temperament, color in the voice, and agility or flexibility. When first learning how to sing, most women start with that middle voice, that mezzo soprano. With training and exploration, you learn to stretch your voice– in both directions. You find out what feels comfortable, then begin to develop your repertoire.

Porcupine: Whether it's an opera, an operetta, or an American musical comedy, you sometimes spend hours in roles that might extend over weeks or months. On stage, does your mind ever wander?

Benson: I never let it. Because the way I look at it, every audience is a paying audience. They deserve the best I can give at that moment in time. There are probably people out there who have never seen the show before, never heard or seen an opera. That it's a new experience for them, I always felt a great responsibility to them and to the art form. I had to be focused. I always had a natural acting talent. But because I didn't always have the natural voice, I had to work very hard, technically, to remain in control. And I was so curious, so determined to observe my colleagues, to learn every role. Even in college.

Porcupine: After the Master's Degree program at the University of Minnesota, you continued on with doctoral studies at Ohio State. How did you happen to wind up in Europe?

Benson: At Minnesota, it was Roy Schuessler (1910-1982) who taught me how to breathe, how to sing without damaging my voice or developing too many bad habits. He died in my last year. Wesley Balk was there, at the Minnesota Opera Company, and Vern Sutton to assist with the theatrical side. At Ohio State, it felt wrong to be working on my Doctorate when I had nothing to contribute. At about that same time, I won some competitions and the door was suddenly open for me to go to a summer program in Austria. I took advantage, flew to Europe and stayed for fifteen years.

Porcupine: Tell me about that experience.

Benson: When I look back, I marvel at how naïve I was. I had a dream, and felt I needed to go to the place where opera began. How could I call myself a musician if I hadn't even tried it? Fortunately, my parents were very supportive. My mother was an alto who sang in the Milwaukee Symphony Orchestra Chorus. During World War II and the

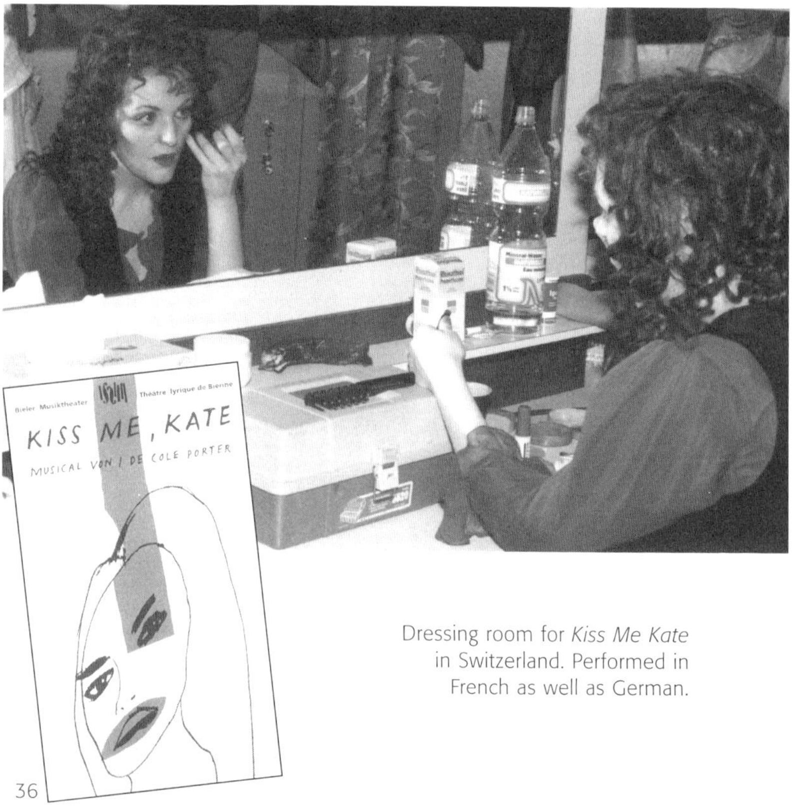

Dressing room for *Kiss Me Kate* in Switzerland. Performed in French as well as German.

Korean War, my father was a tenor in an Air Force quartet called the Air Foursome. One grandmother was an Irish *plinka plinka* pianist, as we called it, my other grandmother the church organist for forty years. So I came from a very musical family.

There's nothing like being thrown into a situation. When I got off the airplane in Austria, I fell in love. I was part of a ten week training program to teach young people how to audition in Europe– German lessons, picking out the right repertoire, how to contact agents... it was such an adventure! I was so anxious to see how people lived in other parts of the world, so attracted to the lifestyle. I knew it wasn't going to be like home. I was in a cold, two room apartment, in a town where I knew no one. I spoke some German, or thought I did. But I made sure I was observant– culturally, as well as musically. I had to learn everything all over again. I'd spend my free time sitting in the outdoor cafés, watching people, listening to them. I knew I needed to speak German like a German.

It's important to know the language– all the semantics, the little nuances. Some say my English has taken on a slight German accent. I've noticed it, as well...

Porcupine: How did the Germans respond?

Benson: In Austria, I was in tears at times. Some nights after rehearsal, I would be so physically tired from concentration, I didn't think I'd be able to get out of bed the next morning. And except for the dialogue, I didn't get a lot of help. Between contracts, when I had no work, I sang on the streets. All that effort, the lonely days and nights, I'm sure I was being tested. But I got tremendous reviews. And I was so attracted to the lifestyle.

When I went to Germany, I got insurance, paid vacations, everything. I was in Koblenz, and it was heaven. That's where I had my first full-time job as a performer. Two years later I went to Kaiserslautern, and in three years began to freelance. I had developed the reputation of someone who could learn quickly and just jump in. I loved the edginess of that.

Porcupine: You married a Czech who was living in Switzerland at the time.

Benson: I'd been in Europe about eight years. I met Viktor at a party– he played rugby for the Zurich rugby team. He was amazed to meet an American who could speak German, and became my biggest fan.

Porcupine: So you brought him home.

Benson: I guess I did. He'd always been curious about life in America.

The atmosphere in Cedarburg is very attractive. Not only because of the arts community here, but also because everything is close– like Europe. We can walk to the bakery, meat market, coffee shops, post office, library...

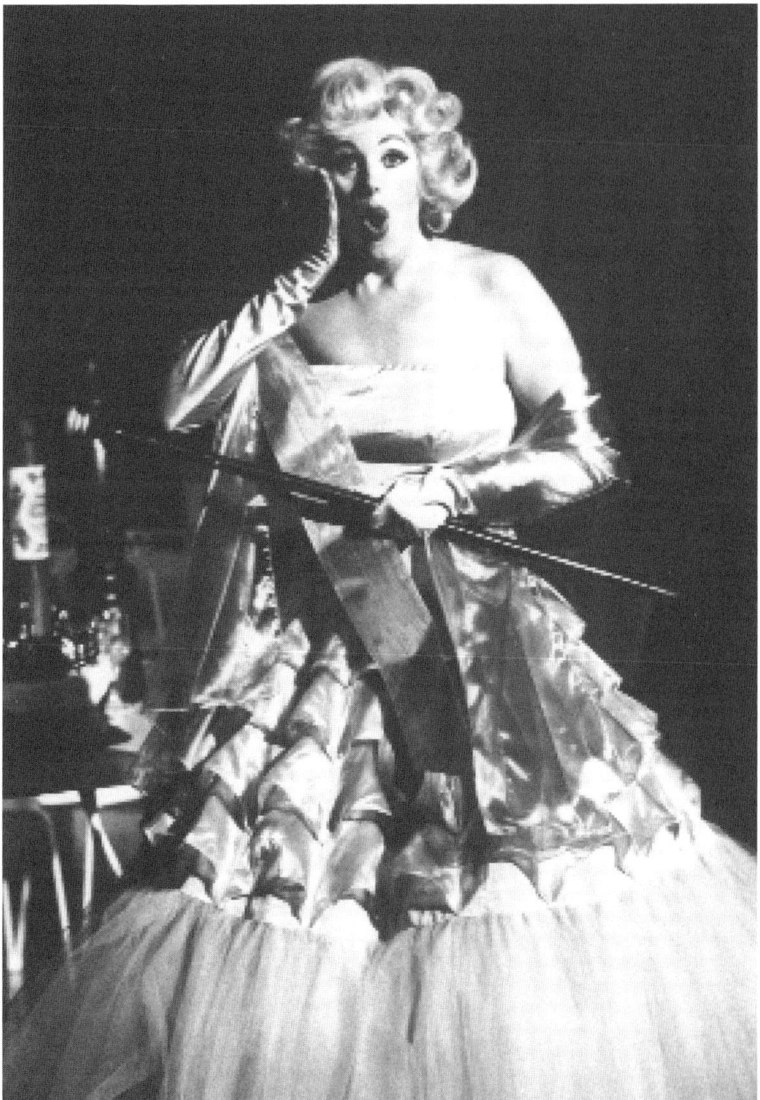

Victoria Benson as Julia *(Der Vetter Aus Dingsda)*, comic operetta, Staats Theatre Kassel– Kassel, Germany

Porcupine: You recently settled down in a small, rural town in southeast Wisconsin. Why did you return? What sort of transition have you had to make?

Benson: My family is here– I was born in Wisconsin, so the transition happened sort of naturally. My mother passed away while I was in Europe. That I couldn't be with her when she died, upset me. Then, when my father fell ill and had a stroke... my husband is Eastern European, and in their culture you take care of your parents. We were already two foreigners, at this time living with our children in Switzerland. We wanted them to know the American side of their family. Professionally, I understood it would be suicide for me. But I'd already had such a wonderful career up to this point. So I said okay, let's do it.

Porcupine: Your father was a Wisconsin state senator.

Benson: From the 28th District. Yeah, he spent a lot of time in Madison. We had a weekend father.

Porcupine: Tell me about childhood.

Benson: I have two brothers and one sister. I'm the second child, the one who seeks harmony in the family. We grew up in Franksville in Racine County, on an old farm. I had a terrific childhood. We were in 4-H, and our 4-H club had a chorus. So I was raised singing and playing in a sort of open, creative environment. My mother saw to that. We would have these political rallies on the farm, with the band playing and people giving the speeches. My grandmother was John F. Kennedy's Midwest campaign manager. So I grew up in a very socially active family. If you had asked my mother, I'm sure she would have said it was tough having my dad coming and going.

Porcupine: Who were your early influences?

Benson: Musically, my immediate family. I was probably four or five, and my parents had just gotten this console stereo. My mother was playing a record by Marian Anderson, who was the first African American to sing at the Met. She had this deep alto voice. When I heard it, I came down the stairs and peeked around the corner. I saw my mother sitting there, crying as she listened. I thought, *why is my mom crying?* So I sat on the step and listened. I remember thinking: *wow, singing can make people cry?* And it made such a huge impression on me– I still remember it so vividly, believing that maybe I could do that some day.

And my parents always sang around the house. We'd go for car rides, and everybody would be singing and Mom and Dad would be harmonizing. I don't want to paint the picture

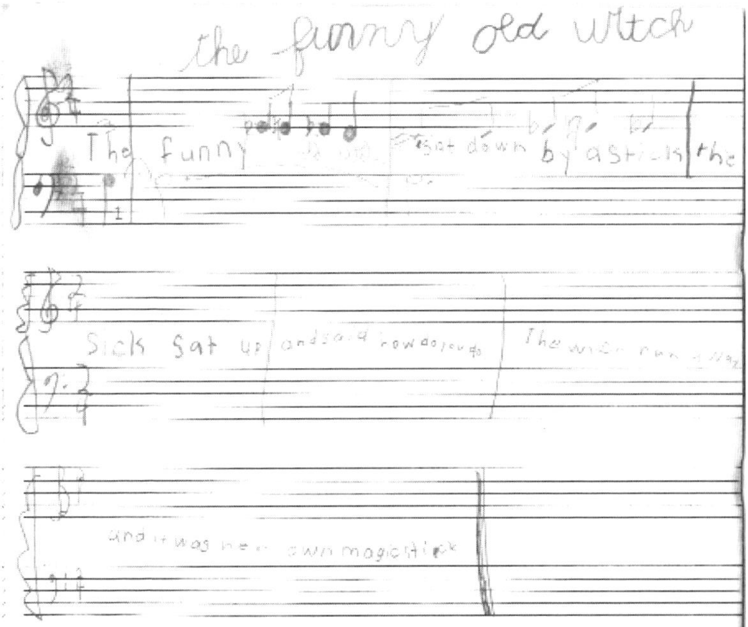

Piano Lessons, Age 7– attempting to write a song.

that we were the von Trapp family, it doesn't quite go that far. Because my parents weren't like stage parents. They just loved music. I probably had the worst voice of all the siblings, but I was the one crazy enough to pursue it.

Porcupine: And now you're a mother.

Benson: Yes. Two boys, seven and ten. Lots of crying and lonely moments when my first child was born. I was happy to have a child, he was a terrific baby. And I had a good relationship with my husband. Everything was right, but I'd lost my freedom. I'd get a call, *can you come and sing? I can't, I just had a baby three weeks ago.*

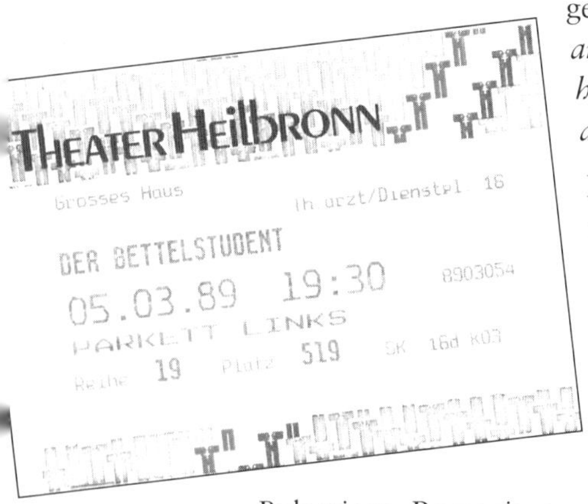

It stopped. It stopped! I found out if you get out of the routine, you're forgotten. Because by this time the Berlin Wall had come down, and there was this huge influx of Russians, Bulgarians, Romanians, who were willing to sing for very little money. They saturated the market. So I had to work really hard to keep my contacts fresh, and to find new opportunities. But I got into the motherhood thing. I settled into that. This was in Switzerland, long before we ever though about coming back to the United States.

Porcupine: Here in Wisconsin, on top of motherhood, you're caring for your dad. He lives with you in your home?

Benson: Yes.

Porcupine: The between generation.

Benson: I'm a prime example, dealing with the three levels.

...Milwaukee is a well-kept secret, I think. There's some amazing talent and theatre work that goes on in this town.

Porcupine: As a singer, is it difficult to see your roles change over time? Do you find that your voice imposes new limitations?

Benson: After my children were born, my voice changed. It got better! Because I wasn't the center of my universe anymore. Although I was always very aware of my art form and what I was doing, I was never described as a snob or a diva or difficult to work with. But I was much more relaxed in my approach after the children were born. My concentration and my desire to only sing were loosened. I didn't feel I *had* to do this or I would die. I'd sung my Mozart, I'd sung almost all the roles I dreamed I'd do. So I was

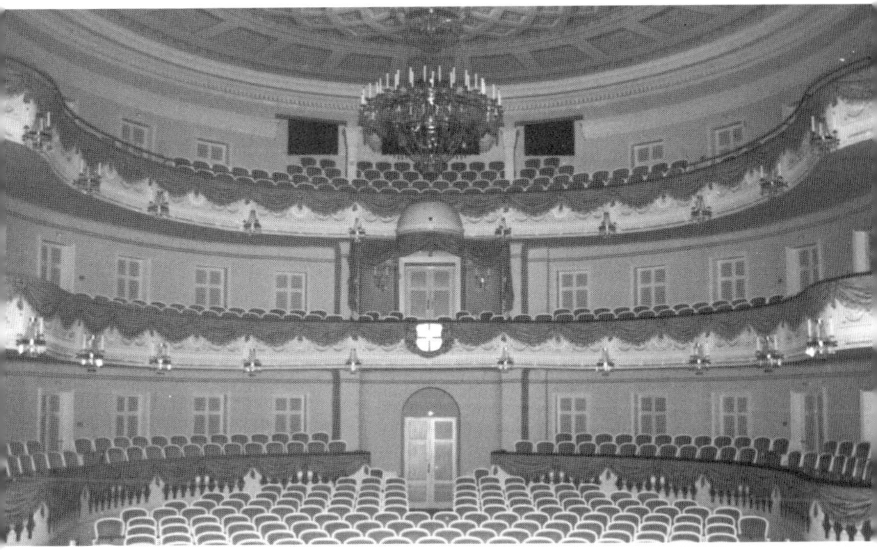

First theatre Victoria sang in. Koblenz, Germany.

willing, and very happy, to take on this turn. I hooked up with new composers, began singing new music. I actually felt *more* in control.

Porcupine: What projects have you found yourself involved in since your return to the Milwaukee area?

Benson: When I first moved here in 2000, I auditioned for Richard Carsey at the Skylight Opera. Because it's what you do– you come to a new place and you audition for the directors. We hit it off right away. Shortly after that, he asked me to do a number of preview concerts to advertise the Skylight's upcoming season. Since then, we've performed together on a number of occasions.

I did a faculty recital at Marquette when I was there, and a concert with the Milwaukee Mandolin Orchestra with whom I'm going to be recording as a guest artist on their next CD. I've sung some preview concerts for the Florentine Opera, recitals at Festa Italiana in their opera tent, sung at the Calatrava...

Porcupine: ...*Romeo and Juliet* at the Skylight Opera.

Benson: Yes, not knowing it would be more acting and dialogue than singing. It was a real learning experience for me. Because I was so used to having the music dictate my parameters of movement and interpretation.

Porcupine: I've heard you suggest that if Shakespeare is the grand form of theatre, then opera is the grand form of music.

Benson: Because Shakespeare is so close to music, with its inherent rhythm and moments of silence.

Porcupine: You see them as a complement to each other?

Benson: Absolutely. There are many, many operas based on Shakespeare– *Othello, Romeo and Juliet...*

Porcupine: But Gounod (composer Charles-François Gounod–1818-1893) took certain liberties. In particular, Juliet wakes up in the tomb and Romeo is still alive. Is it okay that there are characters in the opera that you don't find in Shakespeare?

Benson: If you had asked me that twenty or more years ago, I would have said I'm appalled. Because at heart, I'm a purist. But I think, now, that it's crucial to hook in future generations of listeners.

Gounod's original opera was all music, and followed the complete story of *Romeo and Juliet.* But stage directors and orchestral conductors like to break with tradition, too. At the Skylight, *Romeo and Juliet* is probably one of the boldest productions I've ever been in. The Skylight introduces new works and takes old works and gives them new life, so I really think the production follows the philosophy of the theatre.

Porcupine: Is it all enough to keep you stimulated?

Benson: It has to be. I'm doing things as they come, and as time will allow. I'm not going after it like I used to. Because I can't. We make certain decisions in our lives. But I'm hearing the music in my head, and finding creative opportunities.

Porcupine: You still sound engaged.

Benson: I hope so. I love what I do. I think I've found a sort of balance– between career roles, motherhood, wife and caregiver. Once you get music and performing in your blood, you can't just give them up. Vocally, biologically, my voice– the human voice– is at its peak right now. I'm singing the best I ever have. Oh, well.

W.A. Reed, Cedarburg, Wisconsin, is a poet, novelist, and Managing Editor for *Porcupine Literary Arts Magazine*. His poetry and short fiction have appeared in numerous publications. He is currently at work on his second novel.

Eric Rawson

Poetry

Realist to His Beloved

So it has come to this
    Loneliness spreads its filthy wings
As if summer promised
    Only sweet onions and sunlight
In the bellies of grapes

I Borrow a Page from Spring

I bury this note in the fire
    That I wrote when I was fifteen
About the brookside where I nailed
    My skin to the fern-molded earth

For many years now I have gone
    Without the burning kiss of God
The wind sings a blue-note all night
    Around the shelter of the sleep

I live within I live without
    The beautiful Sanskrit of youth
But still I creep into the world
    And find tiny pearls of birdsong

In the Mean Time

In the mean time the locust skins
    Curl under the curling petals
Their smell like mildewy pages
    The earth dries and the trees hang down

Between now and midnight: the rain
    Will pass in a pounding of hooves
To bed in more deserving towns
    Leaving me to you still droughted

Thinking about Voltaire

Why do I have an apple tree
To light my way?
Black rain falls in my heart
I cheat my friends of love
Am a kind of thief

Yet I sit by the heating vent
Watching t.v.
With a basket of black
Arkansas apples glad
To live in this world

Eric Rawson is from West Hollywood, California. His poems have appeared in numerous periodicals, including *Slate, American Poetry Review, Ploughshares, River Styx,* and *Epoch.*

Richard Thieme

Essay

Ferg's Law

This is how the Internet works:

Somebody in Kentucky finds one of my columns and asks to reprint it in a newsletter. Our email exchange begins a dialogue in this case, on Buddhism, online spirituality, and how the world works and in one of her exchanges, my email pal says, "I have a friend, Jim Ferguson, and this is Ferg's Law:

When everything can go right, it will, and at the best possible moment."

If that's how computer networks work, that's how life works too. Too many bugs or breakdowns or glitches can obscure the bigger picture, that a vast complex network pretty much works pretty much most of the time.

We are pulled in different directions by conflicting evidence. Jokes abound about differences between optimists and pessimists. But this is deeper than that. This is about the tentative conclusions on which we base the way we live our lives. If the evidence were simple, our decisions would be simple too.

This weekend I am in Iowa for a family funeral. It was funeral weather, overcast and cold. We walked through snow to a hole in the ground and stood shivering in the zero wind as final goodbyes were said. I have attended dozens, no, hundreds of funerals, and always there is a desire for some sign from beyond the grave. And always there is silence, the answer to our questions is silence, and finally the silence becomes the question to which we must discover our own answers.

Do you ever get sick and tired of the negativity, the whining and complaining about the Internet, computer technology, and where the world is headed? Negativity is a mode of control, a way to try to make people, places, and things fit into a manageable box that we can sit on or manipulate.

I guess we need to live within safe boundaries.

I was diving once in an isolated bay on Maui, far beyond Kapalua, where tourists seldom venture. I was swimming out over the dark corrugated texture of the reef. Toward the mouth of the bay and the open ocean, curtains of blue and deeper blue shimmered in the distance. Suddenly the reef ended and the drop below me was hundreds of feet to a sand bottom. I felt the loss of safety represented by the reef but kept swimming. Then, beyond the curtains of deep blue something moved, something large and dark, so large I didn't know what it was, and the next moment it was gone.

I turned and swam back toward the reef. Once I was over the coral again, fear of that unknown dark form disappeared. The reef represented the safe harbor we are always seeking, while the open water with its unknown possibilities was the invitation of life itself.

It is time to leave our comfortable rooms, the poet Rilke wrote, every corner of which we know, and venture forth into eternity.

Web sites work best that lead us by easy stages from accessible text or images into the complexity of information patterned beyond our comprehension. Our thinking too leads by degrees of precision from simple manageable truths to the highest level of insight.

When the Buddha became concerned that his teaching was at a depth most people would miss, he began salting his stories with "sandbox stuff," the elementary truths we need to remember: Don't hit. Be gentle and respectful. Don't take other people's stuff.

Murphy's law is a true description of life at the lowest level of insight. Things that can go wrong usually do; the tendency to break down seems to be woven into the fabric of all of our projects and woven as well in stars that explode and galaxies that disintegrate. The myth of heat death articulated by physicists, our current high priests of cosmology, turns the silence of the grave into the silence of the universe.

Standing at the grave, I remember a friend, an artist named Jim. He called me from the hospital to say he was dying, but before I could visit, he checked out for a final European trip with his mother and sister. In a tourist hotel in London he lay down and died. They shipped his body back home for burial.

The following week I was discussing plans for a memorial service with his companion. Now, Jim always had long wild hair, shoulder length hair, in keeping with his artist image. As I spoke with his companion, there suddenly emerged on the edge of my consciousness like a stained glass window brightening as the sun came out from behind a cloud Jim's face, and it stayed there, unlike a memory, as the conversation continued. But for whatever reason, his hair was very short.

Then he faded, and moments later, his friend mentioned that to please his mother's conventional sensibility he had cut off all his hair before leaving on that trip.

We can explain that event at any level of precision, but whatever our interpretation, something emerged in my consciousness that told a more precise truth than we usually know how to tell.

Negativity is a way to build a dark familiar reef under our swimming selves. The ultimate source of negativity is a lack of courage and a need to make the darkness safe, rather than risk the open water.

At the graveside and we are always at the graveside the powerful compression of grief tunes our awareness to what matters most. We surrender to the truth that is always there, but buried, our deep longing for forgiveness and mutual forbearance, our desire to surrender the need to be rigid or right. The readiness is everything, and during those moments of exquisite timing tolled by a clock that ticks to a different rhythm we know that when everything can go right, it will, at the best possible moment. We weep, and we embrace one another. The universe is gregarious and welcoming. We are built to live in space that is gateless, unbounded, free.

Richard Thieme is a writer, business consultant, and professional speaker focused on life on the edge, in particular the human dimension of technology and work. He was a contributing editor for *Information Security Magazine* for several years and has been a regular featured speaker for eight years at the Black Hat Briefings and Def Con. He has keynoted security conferences in Israel, Holland, Ireland, and Australia, as well as for venues ranging from Medtronic, Microsoft, and GE Medical Systems, to the FBI, Los Alamos National Laboratory, and the U.S. Department of the Treasury. Thieme's work has been translated into German, Chinese, Japanese, Hebrew, Slovene, Danish, Dutch, and Indonesian. His articles are taught at universities in Europe, Canada, Australia, and the United States. His column, *Islands in the Clickstream*, has been published in Singapore, Toronto, Capetown, Hong Kong, Dublin, Djakarta, and Bangkok, and is distributed to subscribers in more than sixty countries.

Mai Wyn Schantz

Portfolio

Mai Wyn Schantz is a 1999 graduate of Rocky Mountain College of Art & Design in Denver, Colorado. A native of Cedarburg, Wisconsin, she returned four years ago to be closer to her family and the landscape that inspires her work. She is represented by Edgewood Orchard Galleries in Fish Creek, Wisconsin and Grace Chosy Gallery in Madison. Mai Wyn is a co-founder of Artpost Gallery & Studios located in the Historic Grafton Mill in Grafton, Wisconsin.

Each of us has an Up North. It's a time and a place far from the here and now. It's a map on the wall, a dream in the making, a tugging at one's soul. For those who feel the tug, who make the dream happen, who put the map in the packsack and go, the world is never quite the same.

—Sam Cook, *Up North*, 1986

"For fifteen years I've been canoeing the north woods lakes of the Boundary Waters Canoe Area Wilderness and Quetico Provincial Park with my dad. Our summer expeditions are tradition, religion, and the inspiration for most of my paintings. Translating the silent majesty of this wilderness into clean color and smooth brushwork becomes almost meditative, just as paddling is meditative. I travel the gentle curves of a river under overcast skies, I hunker in awe before the foreboding darkness of an impending storm, and I revel in the quiet moment when a dutiful sun drops behind a distant tree line for the night. I live for these moments where everything has significance. I become immersed in the landscape as a visitor and a witness. The rest of the time, and in the studio, I am trying to capture that moment again, to tell its tale, to share my wonderment. Working on aluminum reminds me who I am. It is a reconciliation between opposites: Reflective waters set in harmony to the reflective aluminum surface, an untainted landscape witnessed through twenty-first century eyes."

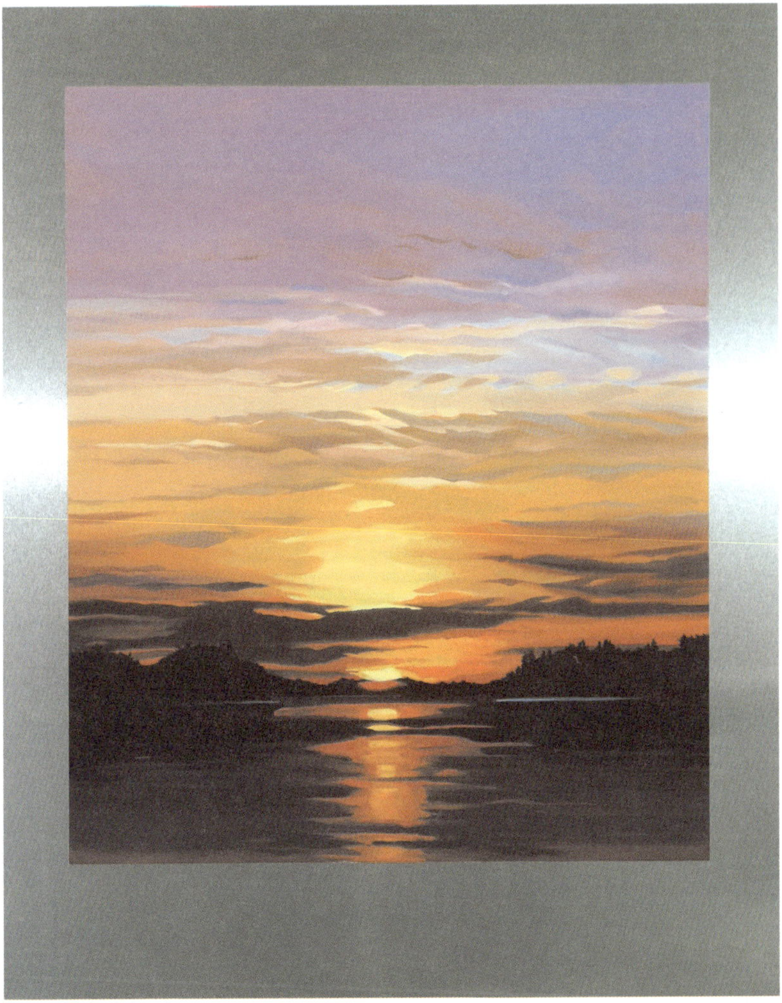

Cache Bay
36" x 30"
Oil on aluminum, 2003

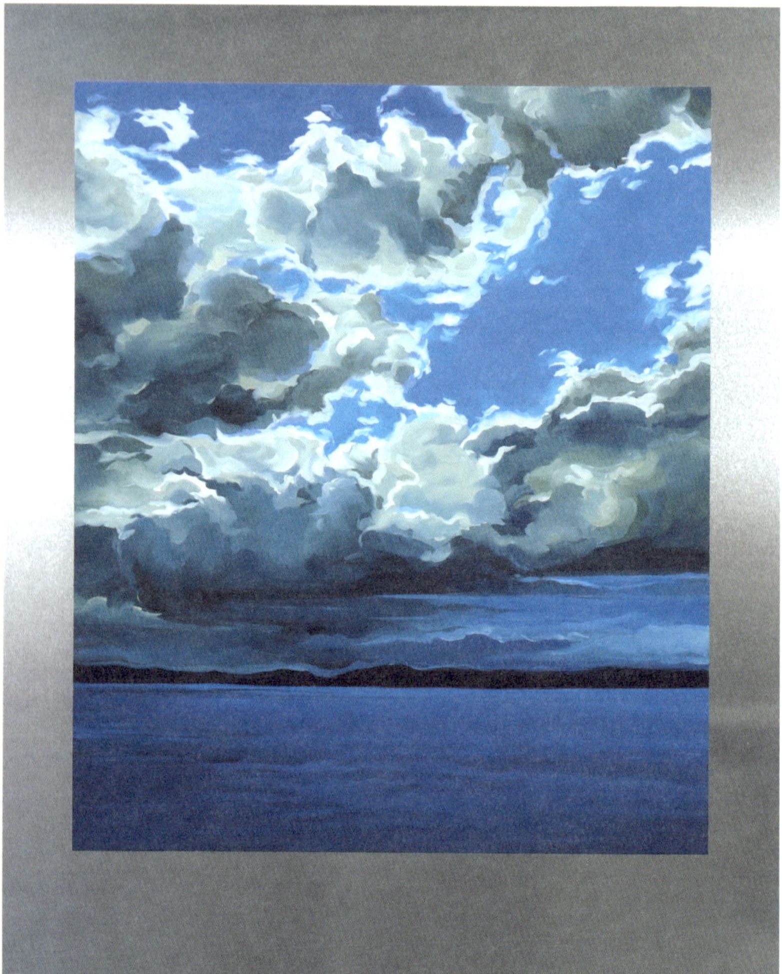

Cloud Break
36" x 30"
Oil on aluminum, 2003

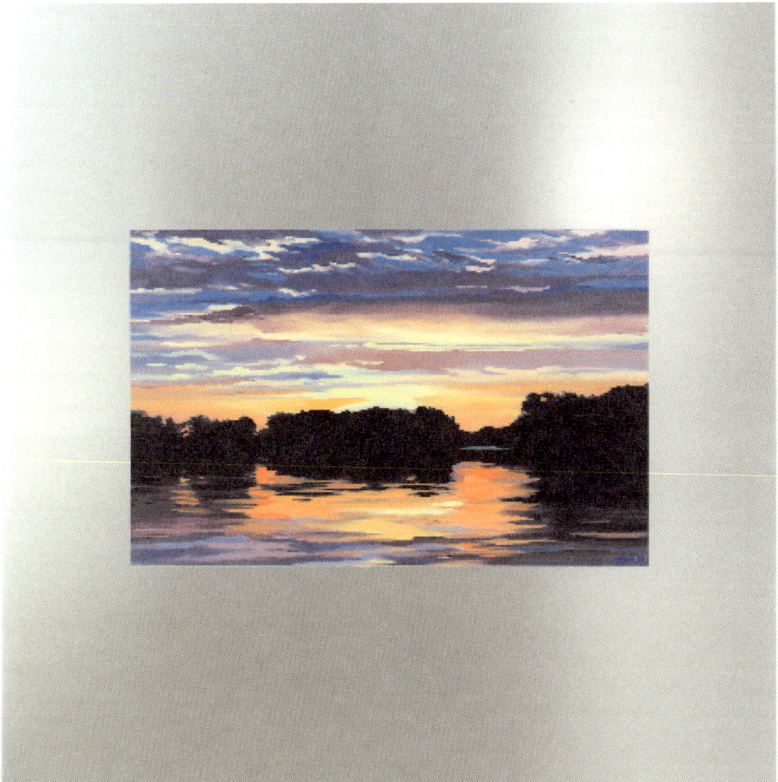

Six Mile Creek Study
24" x 24"
Oil on aluminum, 2003

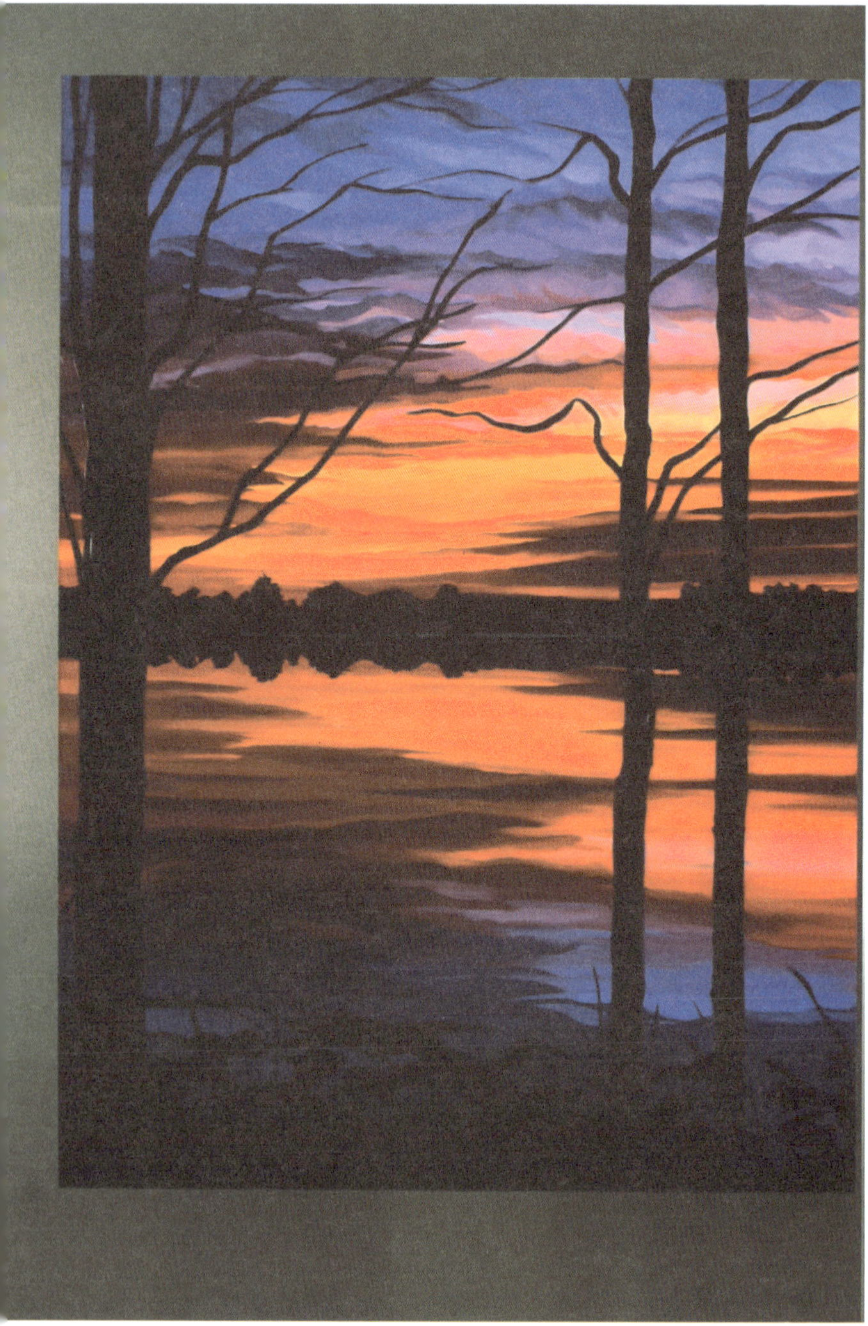

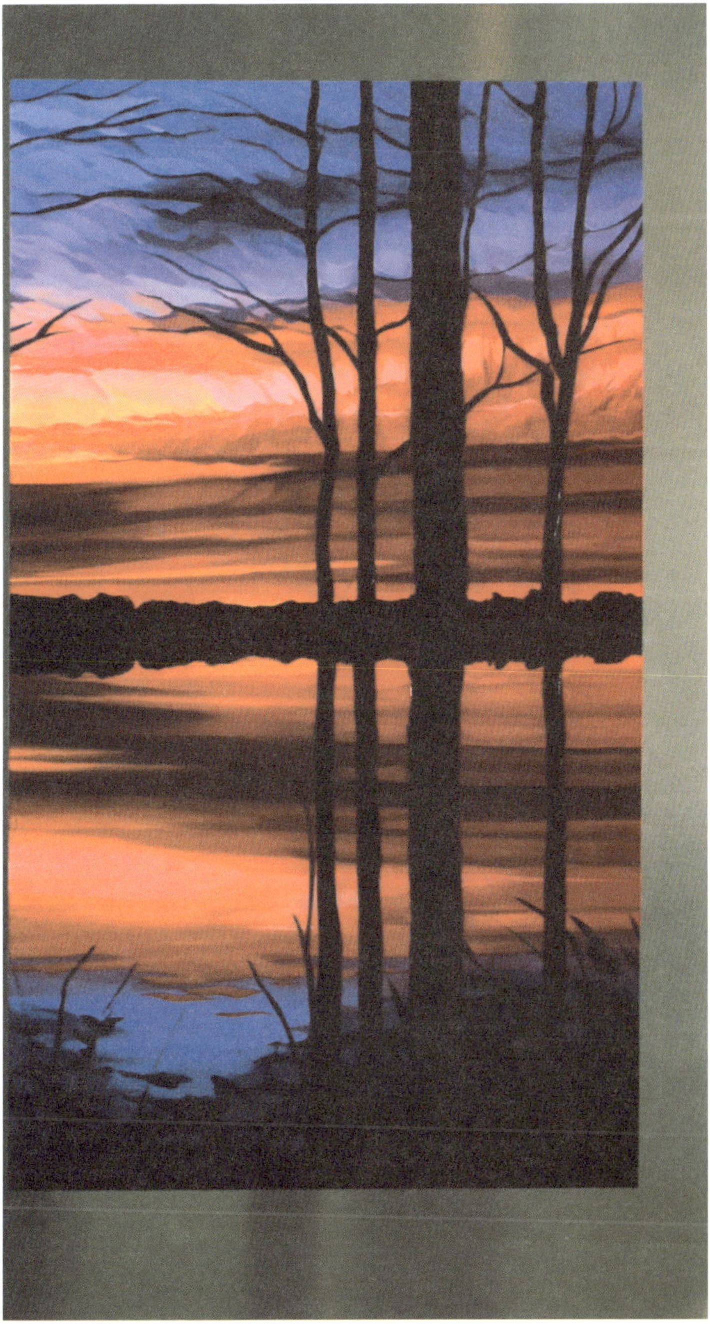

Through the Trees
48" x 60" Oil on aluminum, 2003

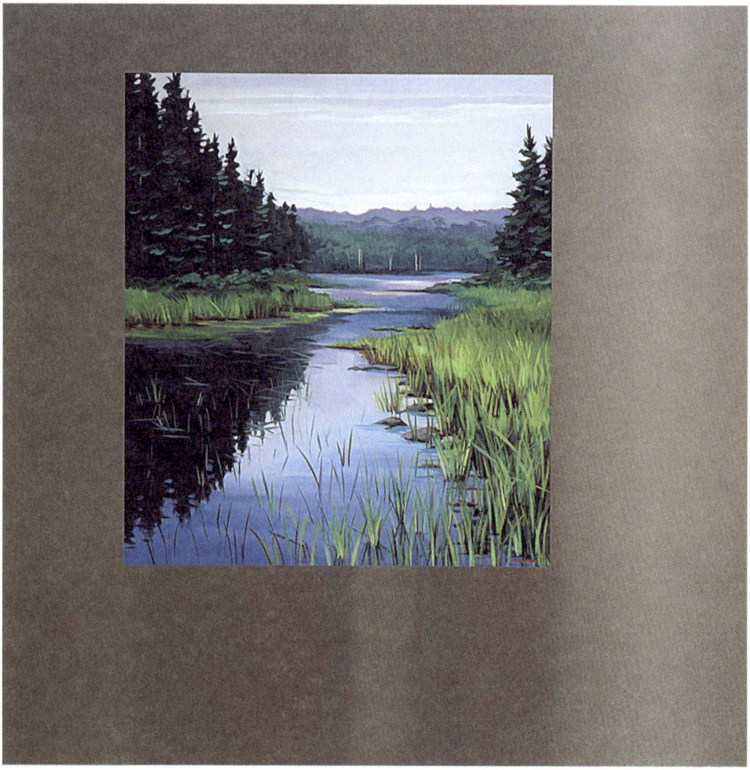

Moose River
30″ x 30″
Oil on aluminum, 2003

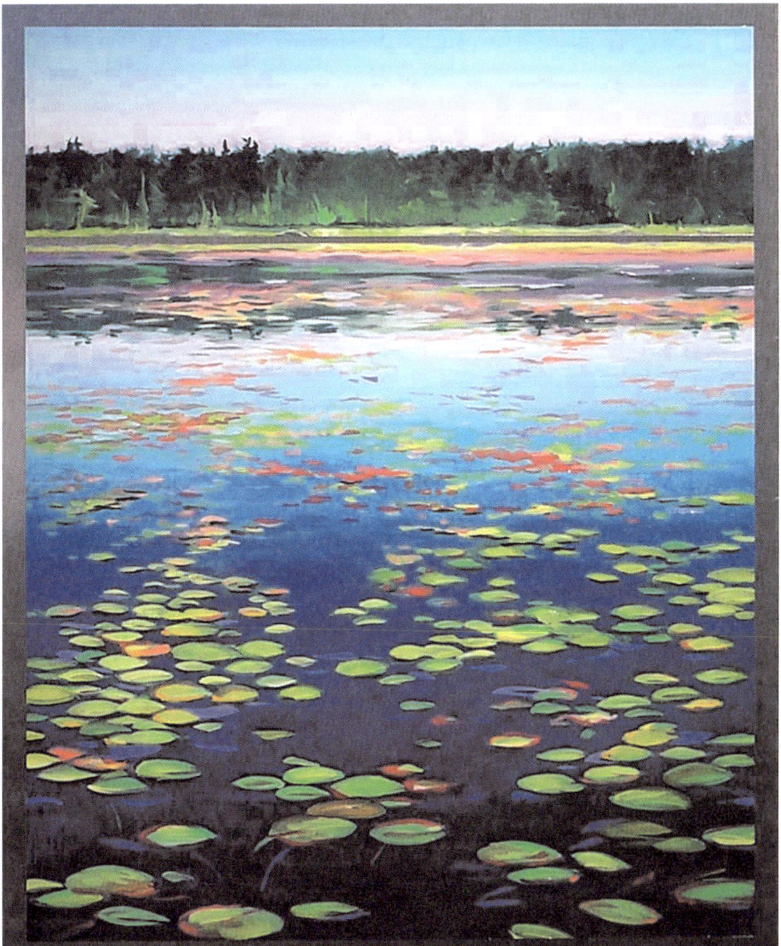

Stuckey Bay
36″ x 30″
Oil on aluminum, 2003

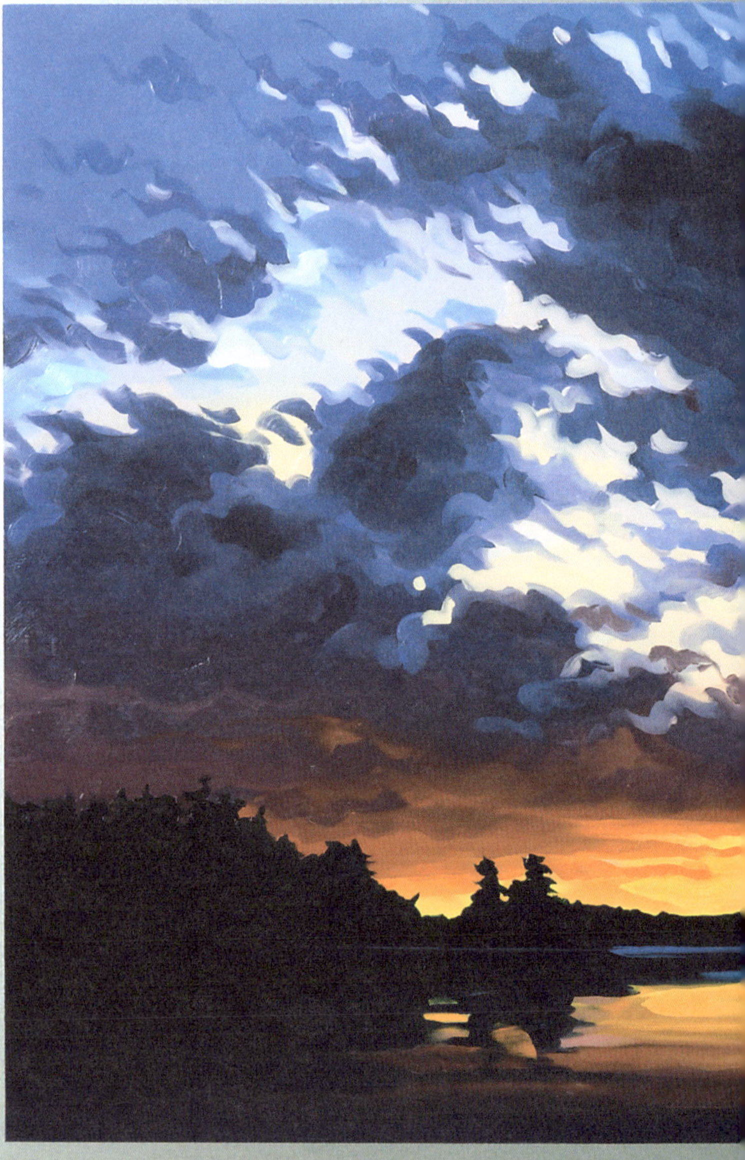

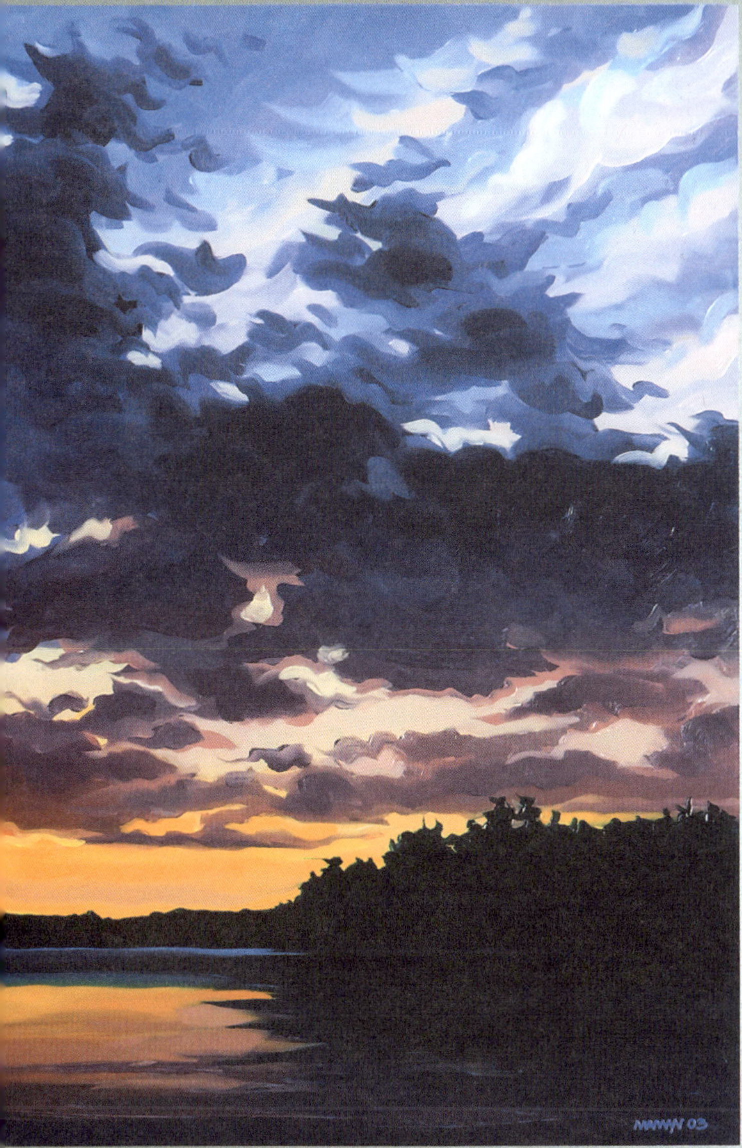

End of the Day
24" x 30"
Oil on aluminum, 2003

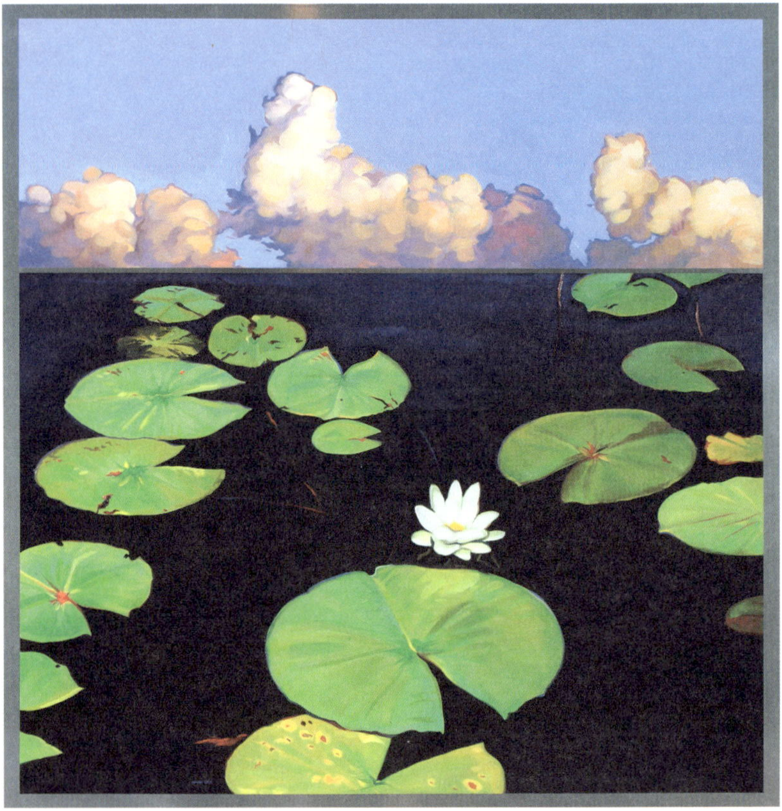

Water Lilies
45″ x 45″
Oil on aluminum, 2003

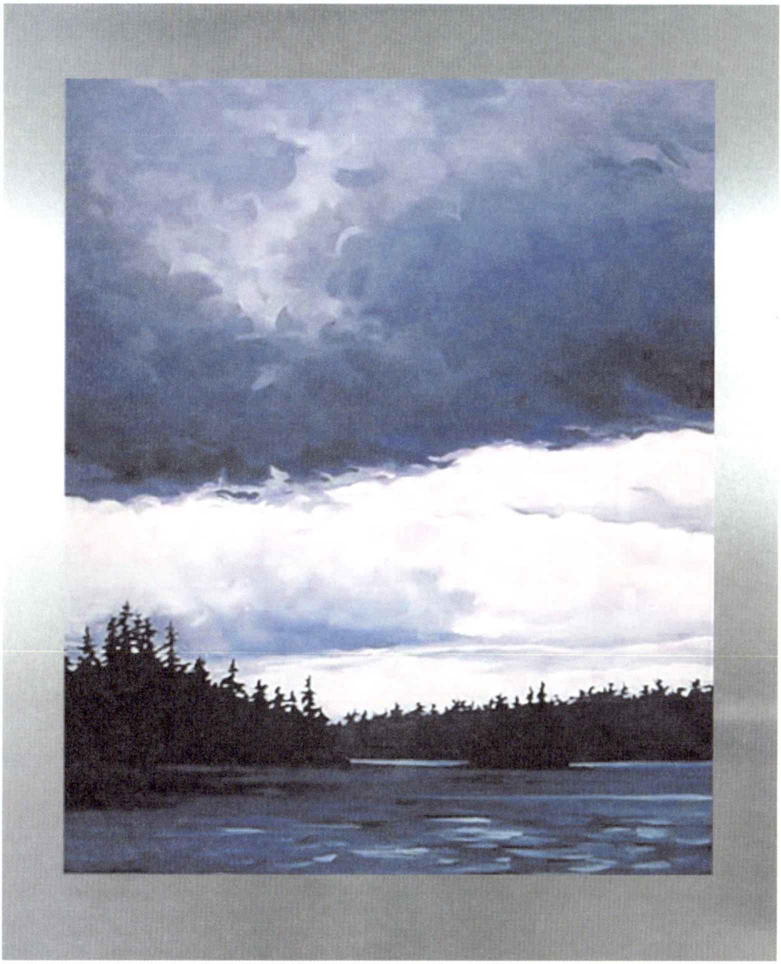

A Change in Weather
36" x 30"
Oil on aluminum, 2003

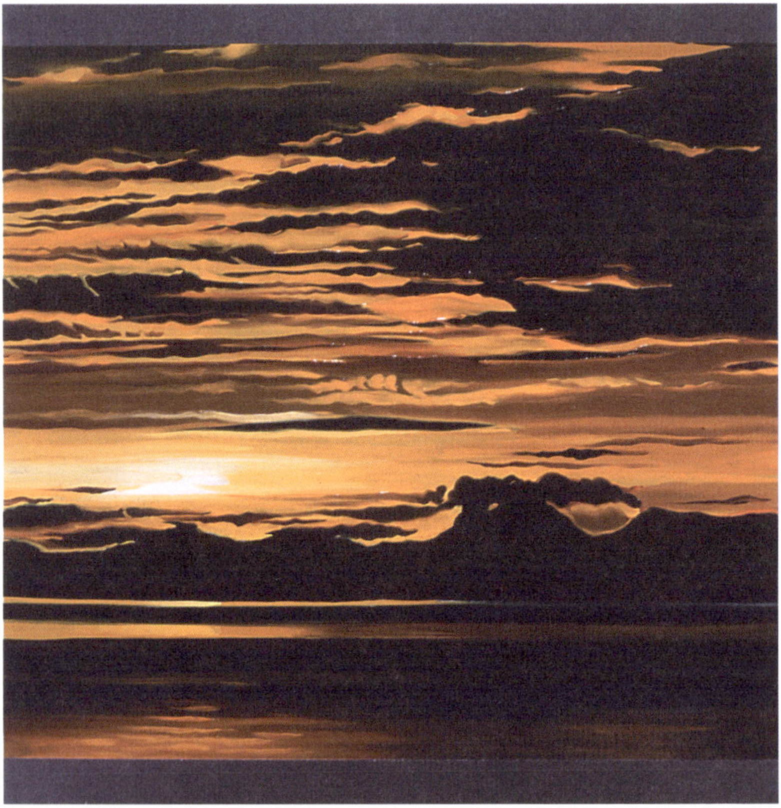

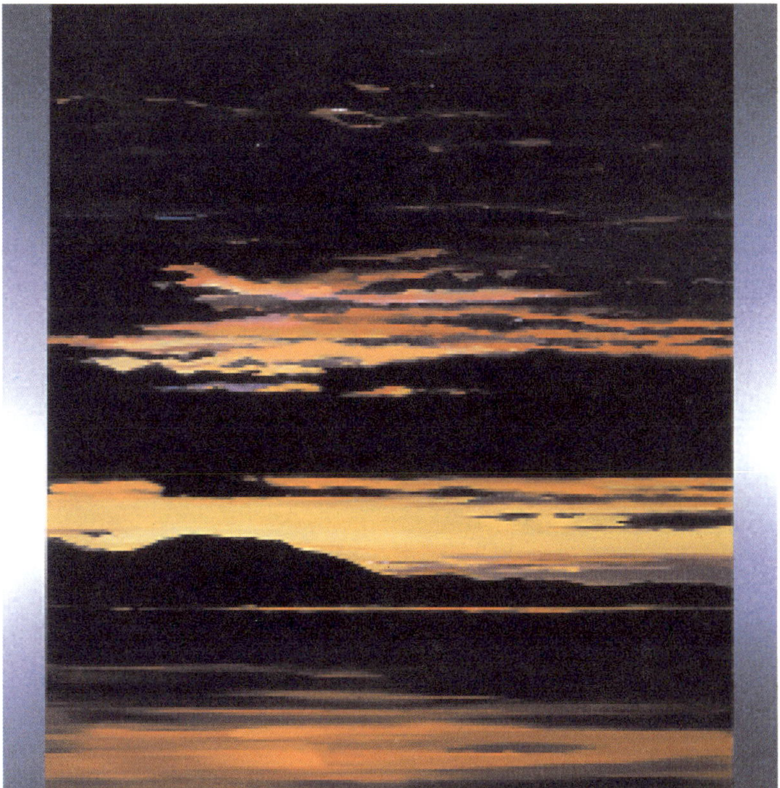

Mystery I, II, III
21" x 21"
Oil on aluminum, 2003

Richard Alan Bunch

Poetry

Red Leaves on a Gray Day

Outside leaves bend slightly, quaver in the breeze.
Green deepens, darkens into red, browns

With each movement.
The day grays, wet. Seasons murmur, pine limbs

Steady yet at the same time dance.
Peace grows cold

As a child cries at gathering clouds.
Green darkens, deepens the autumn hour.

Pines vibrate into undiscovered hues.
Red leaves on a gray day course through

Summits that resound within the sound
Of all returns, upraise the soul

Scale noted heights and unearth
Words devined closest to the breath.

Richard Alan Bunch is the author of *Wading the Russian River, Sacred Space,* and *Rivers of the Sea*. His poetry has appeared in *Cape Rock, Black Moon, Oregon Review,* and *Poetry Nottingham*. He resides with his family in Davis, California.

Halina Duraj

Fiction

The Painting on Florianska Street

When the noon bell rang at the coat factory, Julka punched her timecard and walked directly to the train station. She loved to go to Krakow alone on Saturdays. All afternoon she walked the cobblestone streets that spilled out onto the pigeon-infested squares, and sometimes she bought pastries to snack on– crispy wafer tubes filled with cream, or sugar-glazed buns. Sometimes she stepped into the cathedral on Plac Kosciuszko, and sat in a back pew, relishing the dim, echoing quiet– so beautiful after the relentless thrum of the machines in the sewing hall. Mostly she window-shopped, and dreamed of a new dresser, something dark, mahogany maybe, or black walnut, and a real dining table set, so she could invite Goszka and the other girls from the factory over for dinner parties. But if she bought anything, it was usually something small– a spatula for the kitchen or a doily for the coffee table.

On this particular Saturday, Julka stopped in front of the window of an art gallery on Florianska Street. What had caught her eye was a painting, the size of the upper third of a door. The sun glowed deep red in one corner of the canvas, and radiated orange and yellow light across a marsh. Reeds bowed and waved in a breeze; dark trees stood at the left edge of the canvas. But the reeds weren't green the way she expected reeds to be– they were splashed in the apricot light of the sun. Yes, that was exactly as they would look, with light on them. She stood in front of it– she didn't know how long– trying to figure out if the sun was rising or setting over the marsh.

She walked in, the bell on the door jangling as it swung shut behind her. She turned to the shopkeeper– a balding man slumped behind the counter, smoking a cigarette, the pages of the *Tygodnik* spread out in front of him.

"Excuse me, sir. How much is this painting?" she asked.

He glanced up, then back down at the newspaper.

"A thousand *zloty*," he said, without looking at her. A month's pay. She had two-hundred, maybe two-hundred fifty *zloty* in her purse, and another hundred in an empty coffee canister in her kitchen, but it still wouldn't be enough. She didn't even bother asking if she could put the painting on lay-away. The store was state-run; the man behind the counter would get paid whether the paintings sat on the walls or not. Julka looked around at the other canvases– mountains and forests, cityscapes, farmland– but her eyes always fell back to the marsh. She stood in front of it until she was embarrassed that she had been in the shop so long. The bell on the door jangled once more as she walked out, and she blinked in the brightness of the street. She was not seeing the sun over the shops and the street and the cars. In her eyes, the sun still poured molten gold over reeds and dark trees.

On Sunday morning, while Julka boiled water for her after-church tea and sliced bread and butter, she glanced out her little kitchen window, and far below, in the sprawling backyard of her apartment building, she saw the top of her landlord's head, his thinning, grayish hair. He was gathering a bouquet of gold and rust-colored chrysanthemums.

The house had once been a farm, on the outskirts of Trzebinia, but now the town spread all around them, and parcels of land had been chopped off, one by one, for tall, dismal concrete housing. But Zielinski's backyard, ringed in alder and birch, was like a little piece of the open countryside, and in the spring, he grew tulips, row after row of them, and chrysanthemums in the fall. On Saturdays, he sold bouquets at a table he set up in front of the house.

Julka had a hunch the flowers would be for her. He often brought her flowers on weekends, saying they were from his mother, that she would have picked them herself if she could bend over that far. But Julka knew it was an excuse to check up on her in a friendly way. Zielinski had a sort of fatherliness about him, although he had no children and had never married. He was in his mid-forties, a *kavaler*– bachelor– living with his ailing mother.

Julka felt sorry for him– every evening he rode his moped down the block and turned left at the corner to visit a woman who lived on Ulica Jablonksa. Her name was Tosza, and Julka had seen her once, riding on the back of the moped when they passed by the house. She had copper hair in a startling, unnatural shade. It had flown out behind her, most of it protected beneath a scarf tied around her head. Her arms were wrapped tightly around Zielinski's waist, her skin pale against his brown leather jacket. Zielinski had not even looked up at the house, as if he was in a new neighborhood and no house was any more significant to him than any other. A neighbor had once whispered to Julka that Zielinski had been courting Tosza for twenty years now, but his mother forbade him to marry her. Tosza's older sister had divorced her husband– a disgrace to the entire family. The neighbor had said that Zielinski was just waiting for the old woman to die.

Julka didn't believe her. She could see that Zielinski loved his mother. He called her *mamusiu*, as a little boy would, and cooked for her every day when he got home from his job as a clerk at the courthouse. Passing by the open door to Zielinski's apartment, Julka often saw him carrying a carefully loaded dinner tray, complete with a vase of wildflowers from the front garden or whatever blooms were growing in back, into the old woman's bedroom. On their evening walks, Zielinski kept one arm around the old woman's thick waist and one hand under her elbow, supporting her as she hobbled.

But once, nearly a year ago, on a Saturday evening, Julka had come up the stone walkway after spending the afternoon in Krakow, and had heard the old woman shouting, "Stasiu! *Pomusz*!" Julka dropped her satchel in the front hall and burst through the old woman's door. Pani Zielinski lay sprawled on the kitchen floor. Julka tried to lift her but only succeeded in dragging her a few inches. "Find Stasiu," the old woman cried. Zielinski had gone to a nephew's wedding in

Katowice, she said, and he should have been back already.

Julka ran out back to check the yard. "Panie Zielinski, Panie Zielinski," she called, and then she saw him, about halfway down the stretch of the yard, at the edge of the chrysanthemum field. He was crouching on his heels, his back against the trunk of one of the alders. He wore a suit and tie and shiny black shoes. He held a pale pink rosebud between his fingertips. Julka guessed it had been his boutonniere. He twirled it around and around. Standing above him, panting slightly from the sprint, she said, "Your mother fell. She's been calling for you." She could still hear the old woman shouting, "Stasiu, Stasiu!" over and over again.

Zielinski looked up quickly, he pursed his lips, pushed himself up to stand. Only after he jogged up the path did Julka notice he'd ground the rosebud into the tamped earth at her feet, like a tossed cigarette.

Within weeks, Julka forgot that moment, lost in her own life and work and dates. She was grateful that no one told her she could or couldn't go to the theater or out for coffee with one of the boys who courted her. There was a handful of them now– Bogdan, who worked in a bookshop, and Piotrek, the butcher's son, studying to be a teacher. She didn't like any of them enough to marry, but she liked letting them grasp her hand in dark movie theaters, and having them over for tea.

Julka added more water to the little pot boiling on her stove, and when she heard footsteps on the attic stairs, she knew they were Zielinski's boots. Her door was ajar and he poked his head and chest inside, nearly sideways, the rest of his body still hidden by the wall, and thrust the fistful of chrysanthemums out toward her.

"Are you keeping warm up here, Pani Julka?" he asked.

She said, "Yes, thank you," as she filled a vase with water. Her apartment had once been old Pan Zielinski's wood-working shop. It had never been properly set up with heat because in the evenings, when the cold set in, he had escaped to the lower floors. Julka had only a pot-bellied coal stove in the partitioned kitchen, behind the curtain. It was big enough to hold one pot at a time, so that she could not make tea at the same time she cooked soup or boiled sausages, and it did not heat the apartment sufficiently in the winter. She slept under two down comforters in the coldest months.

Despite this nuisance, Julka loved her apartment. Her heaven, she called it. She had grown up in a two-room farmhouse in Zarebki, with five brothers and sisters and a roof made of thatched straw, and nothing had ever been her own. Sometimes at dusk when she was out far enough in the pasture with the two old black cows and the crowded house was far removed, she had turned her back to it and pretended that it was not there. She had been alone then, and pretended everything she could see belonged to her.

Zielinski had been kind enough to repaint her apartment the way she'd always dreamed. She'd seen it in a book about castles– walls covered in pale blue wallpaper and an embossed silver pattern, stripes of curling leaves. But wallpaper was expensive, so Zielinksi covered the formerly white walls in pale blue paint– blue like the sky over Zarebki at dusk– and Julka stenciled the silver leaves in a pattern of stripes.

She had slowly added a faded, second-hand Oriental rug, a huge, highly polished dark wooden armoire with oval-mirrored doors (she had worked extra shifts, sewing coats late into the night for that), and a *tapczan* that folded out for a bed. She had a record player and a box of records– mostly big band orchestras and folk melodies– and two little wooden tables with intricately embroidered doilies on which she now set her china cups and teapot.

"What new riches did Pani Julka bring home to her castle today?" Zielinski asked, his hands in his pockets. He looked around the little room, smiling.

Julka motioned for him to sit on the *tapczan*. She sat on the chair across from him and told him about the beautiful painting in the shop on Florianska Street. She described it for him in detail, closing her eyes and pressing her hands together over her heart. "It was the most beautiful thing I've ever seen," she said. "Do you like paintings?"

"No, I get restless looking at paintings. I would rather stand in an open field, with dirt under my feet and wind in my hair, than in front of a wall."

"I come from the countryside, too. I understand. But I think this painting may have been even more beautiful than any countryside I've ever seen."

"Why didn't you buy it?"

She looked down, stirred her tea with the little silver-plated spoon. "I didn't have enough money. But I'm going to save up for it."

"Well, that's good," he said. "It's good to wait for what you want." Zielinski looked into his own tea and stirred it. Then he said, "Florianska Street? Isn't that near the old marketplace? Now, the marketplace," he said, "they have fine things there. A leather belt or a coat."

Old Mrs. Zielinski's voice drifted up from below. "Stasiu? *Gdzie jestes?*"– where are you? Zielinski put down his spoon, spread his hands out palms up, and glanced at Julka with a half-smile.

As Julka washed the teacups at her little sink, she decided she would not go to the theater with Goszka that night. No, she would eat broth and bread for the next two weeks, maybe some sausage and apples. When she had saved up enough money, she would go to Krakow. Already she knew where she would hang her painting– on the silver and blue wall above the couch. She would go to sleep in the glow of its sunset at night, and wake under its dawn every morning. Her guests would sit beneath it as they drank their tea. She could admire it as she talked to them. These were the thoughts that floated in the back of her mind as she stitched at her machine in the long workday hours, as she drifted off to sleep, as she said her prayers at night, kneeling beneath the expectant wall.

That week, when she passed Zielinski in the stairwell in

the mornings, or saw him working on his moped outside the vine-covered garage, he said, "How is the lady art collector today?" Julka always laughed. One evening she called hello to him from her kitchen window. He was in the backyard, weeding the chrysanthemums on his knees on a flat board to protect his pants from the mud.

"Have you brought home your painting yet, Pani Julka?" he called up.

She shook her head and said, "Two more weeks, *panie*." He shrugged, then waved an arm in front of him, at the rows and rows of blooms– gold and brown and copper and burgundy and yellow. "What do you need a painting for, Pani Julka? Here is your Van Gogh. Here is your Monet."

The next Saturday, after work, she walked straight home. She did not even buy buns. Usually it was hard for her to pass the bakery without popping in, but that day she walked purposefully, with her head high, gave a nod and a wave at Stawski in his apron behind the glass case. No, she would not go to Krakow today, nor the next weekend. But the following one– *then*. She rounded the corner of her block.

Old Mrs. Zielinski sat at the flower stand, bundled up in blankets and shawls, a wool scarf knotted under her hairy chin, and a long row of chrysanthemum bouquets in pickle jars in front of her. She grumbled to Julka that her son had gone off somewhere, had left her out there at the mercy of strangers– her an old woman, sick, dying. Julka hurried up the stairs. She was impatient to wipe down the blue and silver walls and capture the cobwebs in the corners. Next weekend she would scrub the floors and beat the rug out in the backyard. Zielinski would help her carry it down. He would laugh and tease her, but he would do it. She wanted the apartment to be immaculate when her painting came home.

She had just placed her handbag on the table by the door and was opening the doors of the armoire to hang up her coat, when outside a moped revved louder and louder as if coming into the driveway. She went to the window. Zielinksi usually tended his chrysanthemums on Saturday afternoons and did not go out until Saturday evenings when he rode down the street and turned left at the corner.

When she parted the lacc pancls between the two heavy blue velvet curtains, she saw Zielinski gunning his moped up the center of the street. He did not look up at the house, but stared directly ahead, one hand on the handlebars, the other hugging to his chest a brown rectangle, wrapped in paper and string and approximately the size of the upper third of a door.

Julka let the lace panel sway between the outer curtains and turned away. Directly across from her gaped the bareness of the blue and silver wall, a bareness that had not been there before. She placed one hand on her stomach, and hunched over it a little. In a few moments she would remember Tosza's arms tight around Zielinski's jacketed waist, the boutonniere crushed to a pulp in the dirt of the backyard. But not yet. For now, she would hold her hand to her belly and would press it in hard, as if ensuring the fastening there of a resolve to keep to herself from now on the deepest desires of her heart.

Halina Duraj is a graduate of the creative writing program at the University of California, Davis. Her short stories have appeared in *Pangolin Papers, Floating Holiday,* and *The Acorn*. She lives in Davis, California.

Susan Hazen-Hammond

Poetry

On Seeing Two Paintings

The first, by Cezanne, *Bathers*:
Their skin bare, a dozen women
with full, high breasts
sit near the banks of a French lake
or squat or lie or walk in blue tones
through blue air past blue leaves.

Two women stare at the water.
Another, draped at the waist,
leans her back against bark
and looks away from the lake.
Some warm their hands in the smoke
from a campfire.

A half-painted shape that may be a man
peers at an angle from behind a trunk.
Another stares at the hinge of a woman's legs.

In the second painting, *Echoes*,
not by Cezanne, five women on a dock
at a desert lake take off their clothes.
It is night. An orange light from the shore
shines on breasts, cacti, thighs.

The women are calling to a woman
who stands, stiff and clothed,
at the end of the dock.

Beyond the light, the water is black.
The woman has turned and faces the night.
A fire inside her shines through her clothes.
Smoke seeps from her shirt
and the legs of her shorts.

Among the pilings below the dock,
a man leers up through the boards,
his face lit in orange stripes.

Cezanne brushed the first scene onto canvas.
Life smeared the second into my cells.

Bathers. Echoes.
Day. Night.

Haystack Rock

Today the fog
hides the haystack
and leaves
the waves
free.

There's no
rock island here,
my eyes say.
There is only the sand.
There is only the fog.
There is only the sea.

This shore
these waves
this fog—
inside my skin
I carry the sea.

Susan Hazen-Hammond lives in New Mexico. She is the author of nine books, including *Spider Woman's Web* (Penguin Putnam).

Peter Schwartz

Poetry

alias

I must mourn my way back
to the box of who
and lay my head upon that crucible

and let the memories drain down
to whatever bleeds best

for some nights are not for romance
but for the quiet medicine of passing

the amputee

now, will you take your lessons away from a thimble
and let the sickle fall
perhaps leave a finger in the doorway
as bait
for what is after all
a trickle too late

or will you wait for the gourd's worth
forsaking that half a friend
for what never was
a promise to depend on
but in

will you unsheathe absolutes
right up to the wrist
for nothing more than mist
for this

or will you mirror a shadow
for the sake of that stranger's looks

such danger
is ritual

will you do
will you denounce

for an ounce of flesh is not a pound
and the foundries need sundries
to scrutinize like lice
in the fleece and flax
before releasing back

will you do
the most blue thing you can
if only to understand

bird call

the old words return
as pigeons from the graveyard
headed for the grapevine

pelting the curtain kamikaze style
with phoenix blood for ink
and nothing forgotten in the turbulence

faith on impact decides
which bullseyes were doves
with half a sunset showing

Peter Schwartz, Augusta, Maine, has traveled and lived in many places including Israel and Egypt. He has been published or has poems pending in *Barbaric Yawp, Curbside Review, Red Owl, Muuna Takeena*, among others. He was chosen for distinguished achievement by the International Association of Paradoxism and is a proud member of the American Academy of Poets.

Barbi Schulick

Essay

The Pine Siskin

When he was a small boy, my son Geremy loved small creatures. He'd take joy in catching a cricket in his cupped hands, then make a show of letting it go, hopping when it hopped, following it into the tall grass until he lost sight of it. He traveled our yard with his head down, his big dark eyes hunting for anything moving at ground level. I was forever piercing holes in jar tops to supply airflow for his spiders and their prey. Soon he moved on to toads, and he had an eye for them— locating one hunched and brown among autumn leaves, scooping another out from the dirt behind the front steps. He kept two as pets: "Toader" and "Toaderette." When they peed in his palm, he'd yelp and toss them to the kitchen floor. I constructed a chicken wire cage for them in the backyard, digging it two feet under so they could hibernate for the winter.

When Geremy was eight or nine, he discovered birds. I didn't fully witness his love for them emerging, didn't notice the first moment he marveled at a chickadee cracking a seed against a branch or caught sight of the flash of red inside a blackbird's wing. But more often, it seemed, his gaze focused upwards and out came the binoculars, field guides, birding journals.

Geremy was a thin, slight boy with a shy sweetness that placed him barely on the edge of his grade school's in-crowd. His lack of competitive spirit confined him to the bench in Little League. He was one to do puzzles, to painstakingly sort and categorize his baseball cards, to read the Nintendo guideline booklet cover to cover, and to watch birds— for hours— outside the kitchen window, keeping track in his journal of how many goldfinch came at what time, whether they were male or female, whether there were babies, and describing how they scattered with the arrival of a blue jay.

I remember a spring when a flock of pine siskins frequented the feeders. Geremy loved how miniature they were, even smaller than juncos and chipping sparrows. The thin, brown-speckled wisps of their bodies balanced on legs slighter than toothpicks. He longed to know them better, and so after school each day, he stood on the deck in front of the feeders, holding black oil sunflower seeds in his outstretched hand. At first his arrival sent dozens of birds away from the feeders and nearby bushes, flapping their tiny wings in alarmed retreat. But gradually the group swooped back, in what seemed a corporate decision to ignore the small human holding out seeds. Geremy stayed put, applying his trademark patience, moving only to wave off a mosquito now and then. And I'd watch, wishing with a mother's fervor that a bird would come to him but never surprised that one didn't. Eventually I'd announce dinner, and he'd plod in, dragging his feet, vowing not to give up.

The afternoon the pine siskin perched on his hand, I was cooking something demanding: a sauce that mustn't boil, a stir-fry to constantly stir, food that should be eaten right away, and so, as I turned off the stove burners, I yelled: "Geremy, come in now, it's dinner!"

Then setting the table in a flurry, I yelled again: "Geremy. Dinner!"

And while pouring drinks: "Geremy!"

"Quiet!" came an urgent whisper from behind me. I turned to find my husband staring out the glass swing set door at Geremy on the deck. There, our little bird of a son was standing straight as a soldier, one thin arm shooting out at a perfect right angle. As if in salute, his palm was upturned, the long fingers flattened together to form a platform for a tiny, brown pine siskin that stood equally erect and looked back at him.

I studied Geremy from the kitchen for those three, four, maybe five seconds, and although he appeared so still that even his breath was halted, I could detect a gentle tilt in his stance, his head and torso reaching delicately towards the bird at the edge of his unmoving arm. It was a yielding that spoke of reverence, recognition, of the sort of hospitality a flower might offer a butterfly. He had become a place for a pine siskin to rest.

When the bird finally flew, Geremy's breath shuddered through him, returning in a grateful rush. He turned to look at us. Sweat had formed on his upper lip, his cheeks were flaming, and I saw wisdom in his young eyes. Through the coming weeks, he would describe over and over how it felt to be so close to the bird, to feel it buoyant, almost weightless, on his fingers. And though he'd try again to woo one, he'd never be successful, so that those few seconds with a pine siskin, his siskin, would be held in memory and heart, the way one remembers words from God issuing through a breeze.

Barbi Schulick writes, cares for her family, and tutors high school students in southeastern Vermont. Her work has been published in *Yoga Journal, Spirituality and Health, A Chrysalis Reader* and *A Real Life*, and has been aired on National Public Radio affiliate WFCR in Amherst, Massachusetts. "Geremy is now twenty-three years old and 6'3". The last time he was home, he spotted a new flock of birds alighting the snow-covered lilac outside our kitchen window. Watching this long, lean man dash for the same dog-eared *Stokes Field Guide* he devoured as a child and rifle through its pages was thrilling. 'Redpole!' he yelled. 'They rarely come to Vermont. Like the Siskins!'"

Rebecca Lilly

Haiku

Her chair creaks, sitting
down— the fat lady dithers
in the lakeside heat

Wind eases; yellow
birch leaves intersperse the green—
the field gleams with heat

Graveyard bouquets blown
about the headstone shadows...
the frozen urns hold

A sagging barn floor
in dusk sun; only starlings
have foothold enough

Down sycamore trunks
raindrops run after the storm...
no noise from wood ducks

A distant train horn...
pale morning moon traced with clouds
through late summer corn

A pause in my thoughts—
from the woods, stream runs as leaves
keep tumbling along

Train rattles to a halt—
shadows of platform strangers
through revolving doors

As surf rolls, one oar
drops free of the rowboat;
gulls cry from the shoals

Cows stand in the mud
of flooded fields; frosted still
of dusk where grass ends

Rebecca Lilly, Port Republic, Virginia, has published two collections of poems, *You Want to Sell Me a Small Antique* (Gibbs Smith), and *Shadwell Hills* (Birch Brook Press), the latter a book of haiku.

Featured Artist

As told to Vicki Reed by Teresa Latrofa
Quotes by Vito Latrofa
Photos by Vicki Reed

Vito's Ristorante:

Giving up is not an option

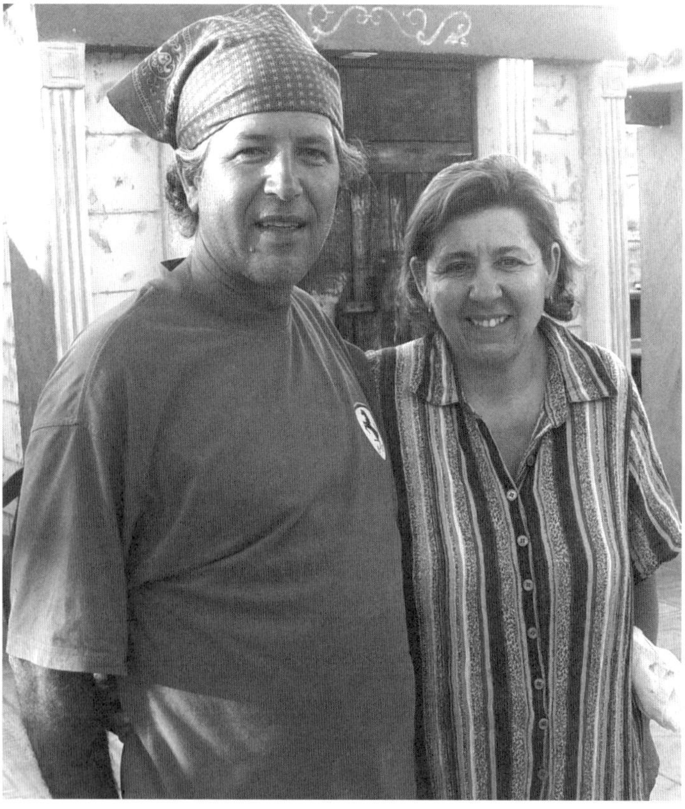

Vito and Teresa Latrofa

I have a passion for cooking just as I had a passion for hairdressing. Hairdressing is an art, you know, and cooking lets me use another artistic part of my brain. —Vito

Sometimes at night we lie in bed and ask each other, "What were we thinking opening an Italian restaurant in a small fishing village in Mexico?" But then we have a wonderful evening with our guests, share food that they enjoy and we realize why we do it. It has always been Vito's dream to cook, to own a small restaurant. My parents owned an Italian restaurant in Winnipeg so I knew how much work it would be. I was not as eager to do it as Vito.

It will be small and we will only have one seating per evening. We'll open four nights per week. How much work could it be?

—Vito

Vito is from Noicattaro in Southern Italy near Bari. My family is Sicilian. Both of our families ended up in Winnipeg. When Vito and three of his siblings arrived in Canada to work in the textile factories in October, 1969, they had never heard of snow. Vito never adjusted to the colder weather so in 1978, after six years of marriage, we moved to Vancouver to be in a more temperate climate. I had worked and put Vito through hairdressing school. In Vancouver he owned his own salon and the last three years of his career worked in the movie industry. I was in banking. We decided we would do something wild and crazy once the children were grown and we didn't have as many financial commitments. We had been coming to this area of Mexico yearly with the kids since they were small. Five years ago we decided to buy a small house in Punta de Mita and make it into a restaurant as well as our home. Back in Vancouver Vito built a small model of how he wanted the restaurant to be. Vito has a vision. He sees things not as they are but as they can be. He drove a rusted heap home one day and said he was going to restore it and drive our daughter to her wedding in it. Although four days before the wedding the engine in "Betsy," the beautifully restored 1956 Pontiac Laurentian, died, he was able to find replacement parts and have it repaired in time for the drive to the church. His vision for Vito's Ristorante was to create the atmosphere of a small neighborhood restaurant in Tuscany. We would build a patio area to serve as the restaurant with an outdoor kitchen and

My mother always baked her bread in a wood-burning oven. Once a week a young man rode to our house on a bike with a wide board attached. My mother then placed her shaped unbaked loaves on the board to be transported to the community's oven for baking. She made enough bread to feed us ten children for one week. I was the youngest and my first job was to sleep at the bottom of two of my sisters' bed to keep their feet warm. I left school after fifth grade to work with my father doing construction and laying water pipes to earn money for the family. I was twelve when my father died and my mother began selling her bread to help support us children. Using a wood-burning oven is the only way to bake bread.

—Vito

wood-burning oven and add a second floor with a balcony to the existing house for our living space.

We let the house sit here for a few years until our older daughter married and our youngest was on her own. The girls were upset with our decision. They complained, "You are not being traditional Italian parents. You are supposed to live close by and help raise your grandchildren."

We sold almost everything and packed what remained of our belongings into Betsy for the drive here. Plumbing and electrical work had to be done before we could move into our house. We needed to stay somewhere while the work was being done so we rented the house on the corner of the street. We had very little with us because you can't fit much into a Pontiac. It was like camping out but the local family we rented the

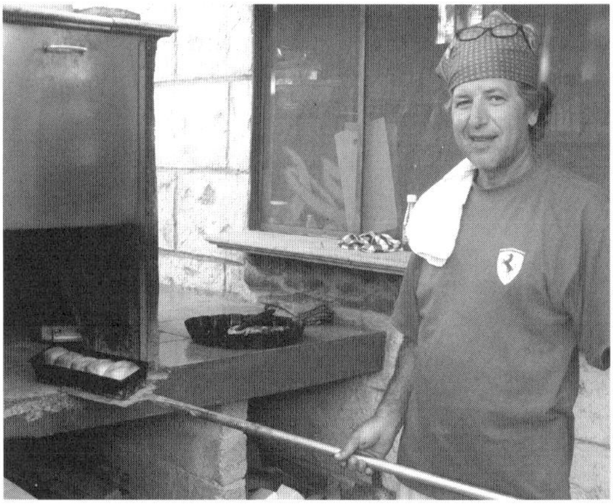

Vito with bread and wood-fired oven

house from thought we were rich. They also thought they could continue to live there with us. In their minds we rented the house and they (twenty-five of them) could still live on the small piece of property as long as they stayed outside of the house. One morning we woke to a pounding sound. One of the women had set up a taco stand and was pounding her tortillas on a board under our bedroom window. When Vito told her that she was by our bedroom she told him not to worry– she would not look in. Another time we heard footsteps on our roof. Vito went to check and found they were having a big party, drinking and looking at the stars. I asked Vito, "How long do we have to live like this?" It was not important that our house had no windows or doors. We could put screens up to cover the openings. All I needed was electricity and a working bathroom to live there. We had been unable to get the plumber to consistently show up to work and thought a deadline would motivate him. We gave notice to the family and told the plumber we had to be in our new house in two weeks. He absolutely had to finish his work by that time. The next day he left town for two weeks.

> *I guess the traditional life is not what we want. When you are parents you are busy in your own separate ways. I was busy working and Teresa was busy with the girls. Now that the girls are grown it is time for Teresa and me to come together again, to become more intimate. It is a great thing.*
>
> *–Vito*

It has been a living nightmare trying to get the local workers to build an Italian-style building. When Vito describes how he wants something done, they say, "That is not how we do things in Mexico." Even after he takes time to explain to them about building arches and columns it is difficult to get them to do it. When building the stairs to the second floor they wanted to pour a huge ramp of cement and then chisel out the steps. Vito wanted to build a frame and pour it all in one stage. After talking to three different people who insisted that that was not the way to build steps he built

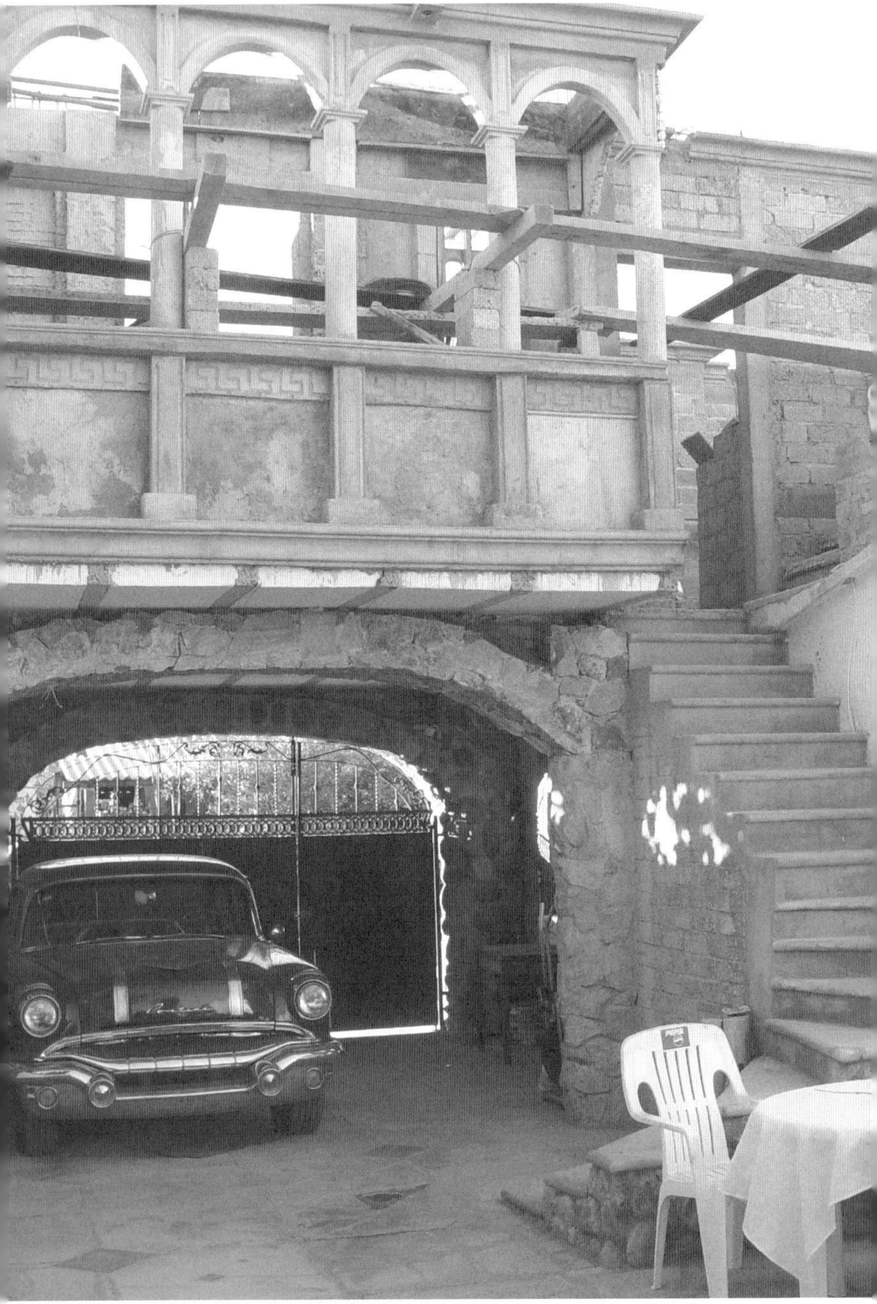

Betsy, stairs and ongoing home construction

the frame and poured the steps himself. The cultures are very similar between Italy and Mexico but the house construction is very different. When placing the river stones in the front wall of the building the workers sorted the rocks and wanted to place same sized rocks in even rows.

I had to explain that you put different sized stones together. You have to let the rocks tell you what rocks they want to be beside.
—Vito

We were planning to open the restaurant in November of 2002 but Hurricane Kenna hit in late October. The nearby resort stole all of our workers to repair their damages so we thought we were never going to open. We puttered away in November and December. Five days before New Year's Eve a friend of ours who runs a nearby bed and breakfast called us. He said he had very special friends coming to stay with them for New Year's and he had a private party that he could not handle. Could we do a favor and host the New Year's Eve party for thirty-five? We still had work to do on the restaurant plus some hurricane damage to repair. We said we were not ready. We didn't even

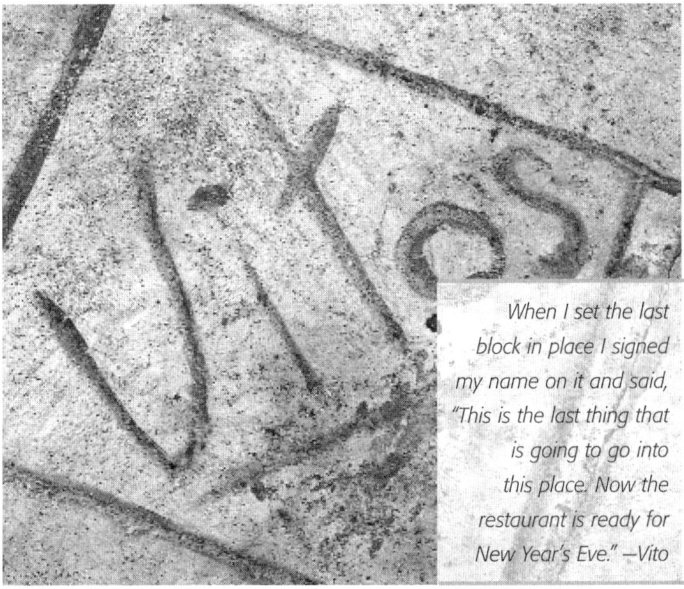

When I set the last block in place I signed my name on it and said, "This is the last thing that is going to go into this place. Now the restaurant is ready for New Year's Eve." —Vito

have dishes. He begged us to do this for him and said he would loan us whatever dishes and silverware he could spare from his own kitchen. He is a really good friend and had done many favors for us. We asked each other, "Do you think we can have this restaurant ready to open in five days?" We began to think we could, so we said yes. We power worked around the clock. I ran into Puerto Vallarta on shopping trips while Vito laid the patio floor.

We had gone three nights with very little sleep and the night before the party we had to cook. I think we cooked until three a.m. I was running back and forth between the outdoor kitchen and the house. Coming out of the house I stumbled and fell on the cement. But when I hit the cement it felt so good to get off my feet, I thought, *I could just cuddle up right here and have a little rest.* Vito found me and asked what I was doing. I said, "I am so tired. I am going to lie here on the cement for awhile just to get off my feet." So that is how we officially opened on New Year's Eve. We had a crowd and all went up on the roof after dinner to watch the local resort's fireworks. We thought we would close again right after the party to finish the rest of our work but everyone had heard we were open and we became so busy with customers we said, "Well, I guess we're officially open!"

On a day when we are open we get up very early in the morning, pack containers with ice and drive an hour into Puerto Vallarta to do our shopping. Because of the heat we put all of the perishable foods on ice. What we are able to find determines what the menu is that day. We have two importers that we depend on to supply us with Italian wine, olive oil, tomatoes, etc. Even so, it is difficult to get what we need sometimes. We have to be home by 1 pm to make the focaccia bread because it takes five hours. Vito does all the cooking because we can't depend on anyone

I don't like to waste food so I only make enough focaccia for the number of guests we have reservations for. Sometimes people show up unexpectedly and it is all gone. They ask, "Where is the focaccia?"
–Vito

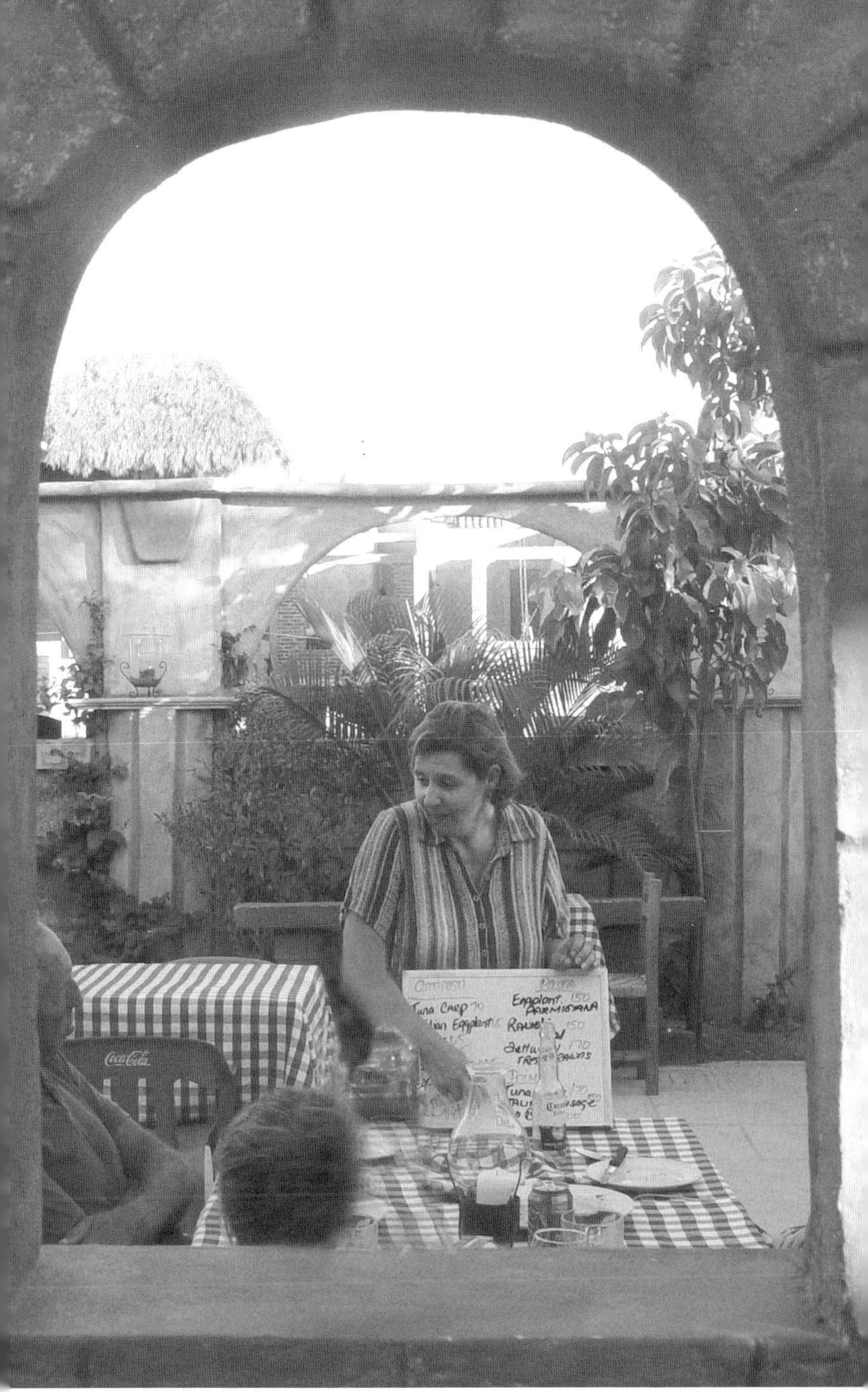

Teresa with menu

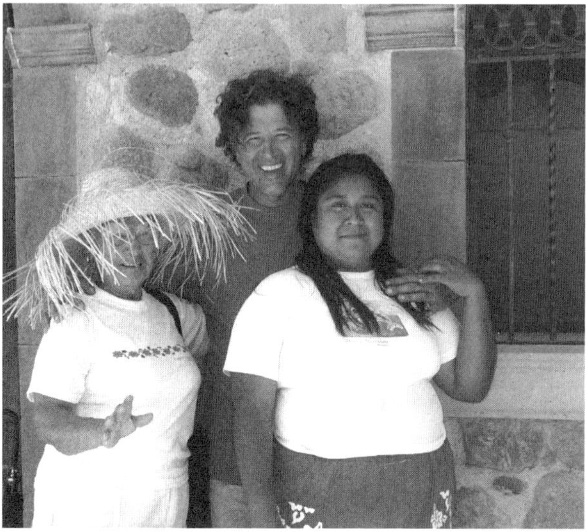

Vito with neighbors Lydia and Anita

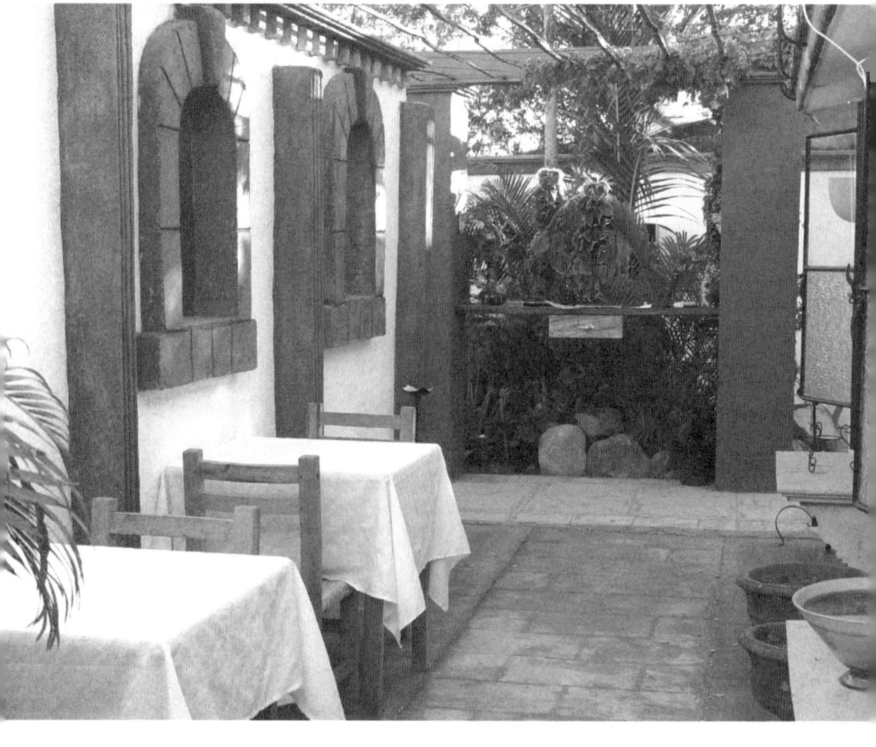

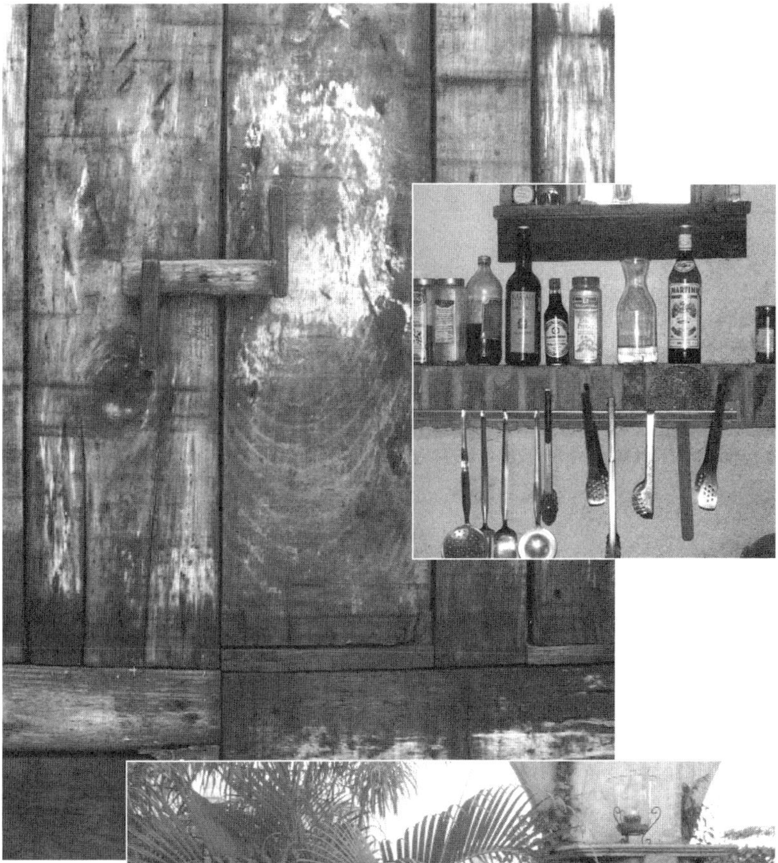

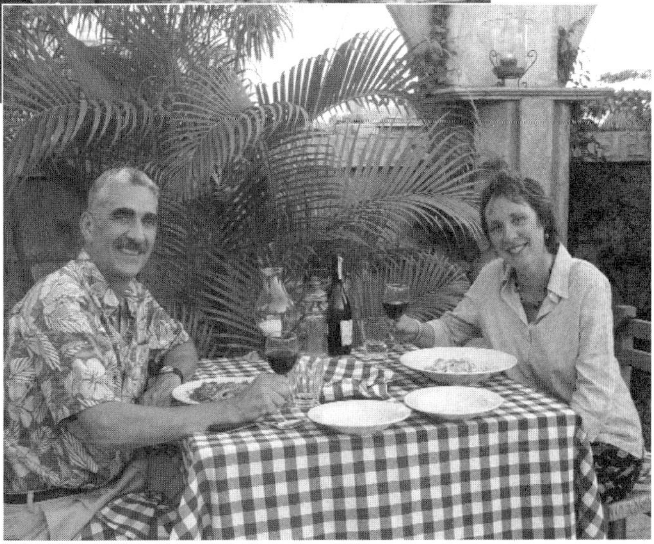

else to show up to work. He does have someone help with the chopping and preparation but if they don't show up, then I am his sous-chef.

Celebrities stay at the nearby resort and come here for dinner. They can be anonymous here, can relax and enjoy the food without worrying about their hair or make up. But some want to be recognized. They ask me if I know who they are and I say no. I don't watch many movies or TV. Vito is more up on those things than I am. As they leave they give me their card and say, "You might want to know who you had dining here." But when I read their name on the card I still don't know who they are. Sometimes after a couple of weeks I become curious and look them up on the Internet. They seem to think they are very important, act strange when I don't recognize them so I feel I should make an effort to find out who they are.

We had a famous rock star here once. He asked if I recognized him and I said no. He said, "It's all about rock and roll, honey." He didn't tell me who he was and I didn't ask. Actually it is all about food. We treat everyone the same, here. Most of our customers ask us not to change a thing but others think we should put a roof over the patio so we could be opened year round– not just during the dry season. But I look at the sky, see all the stars and ask, "How can you improve on that ceiling?"

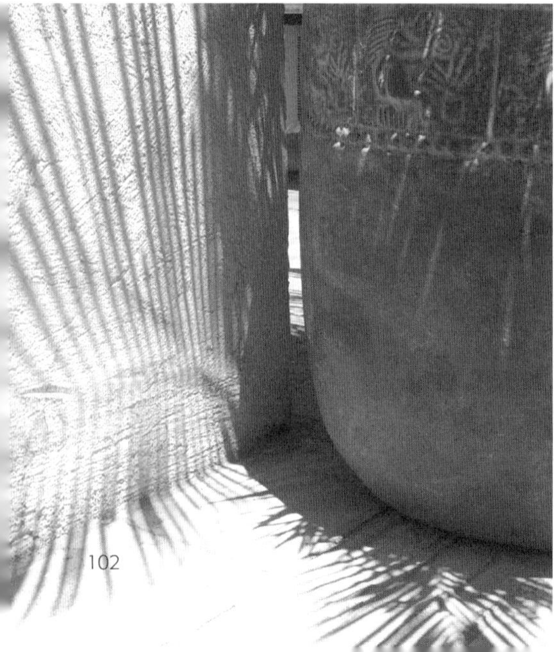

You know, Vito sings and used to have his own band. Our daughter, Vita, when planning

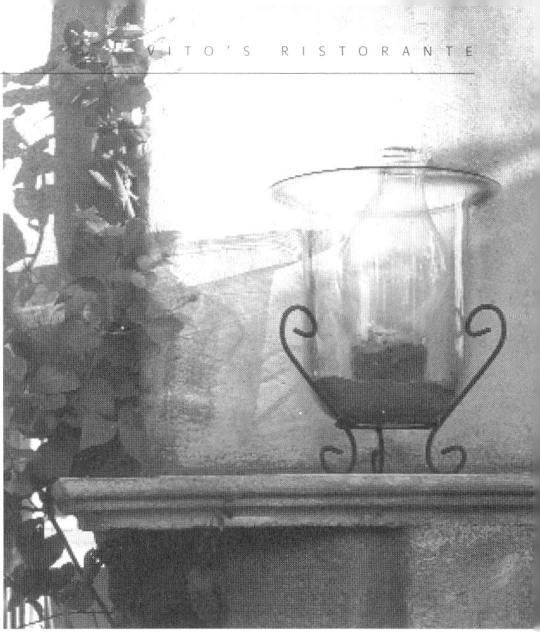

her wedding asked her father what song he had picked out to be played for the traditional father/daughter dance. He told her Stevie Wonder's *You Are the Sunshine of My Life* and she commented that he could have been a little more original. She thought he had not put much thought into this important part of her wedding day. What she didn't know was that Vito had rented a studio and recorded on CD, *Più su* by Renato Zero (a contemporary Italian singer/songwriter). It is a song about a father sharing with his daughter the importance of love, family and friends, with a message of never giving up. He recorded it because he knew he would be too emotional to sing it on the day of her wedding. The recording crew didn't know that Vito used to sing with his own band. When they heard him sing they were so impressed that they called others in to hear what he was doing for his daughter's wedding. I recorded a few words at the beginning of the song telling Vita's new husband that she was conceived in much love and he had big shoes to fill. I think he knew what we meant. At the reception when Vita heard the song she buried her face in her dad's chest. As they danced he sang along with the CD, whispering the words softly in her ear. There was not a dry eye in the place.

I kept telling her to lift her head away from me and smile, this was a very happy time, but she just hugged me tighter. When she was born we almost lost her twice. They were able to bring her back both times. Vita means life. We thought it was an appropriate name.
—Vito

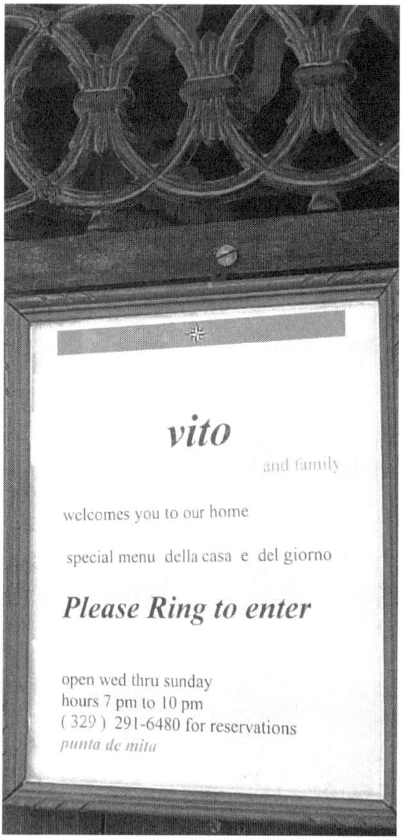

We are rushing to closing time. It is getting lonely. Regulars head north for the summer. No one rings our bell anymore. When the rains come in June we will close for the season and go to Vancouver for our granddaughter Sophia's first birthday. God help us if we should miss that special day. Then we will come back to continue work on the second floor of our house. As we mix cement and work toward finishing our new bedroom and balcony we will reminisce about the many wonderful people we have met over the past year. When some of these people learn of the challenges we have overcome to fulfill this dream of a restaurant they say, "We could never do this." We answer, "Of course you can! When pursuing your dream you just need three things; perseverance, determination and the spirit of never giving up. Giving up is not an option."

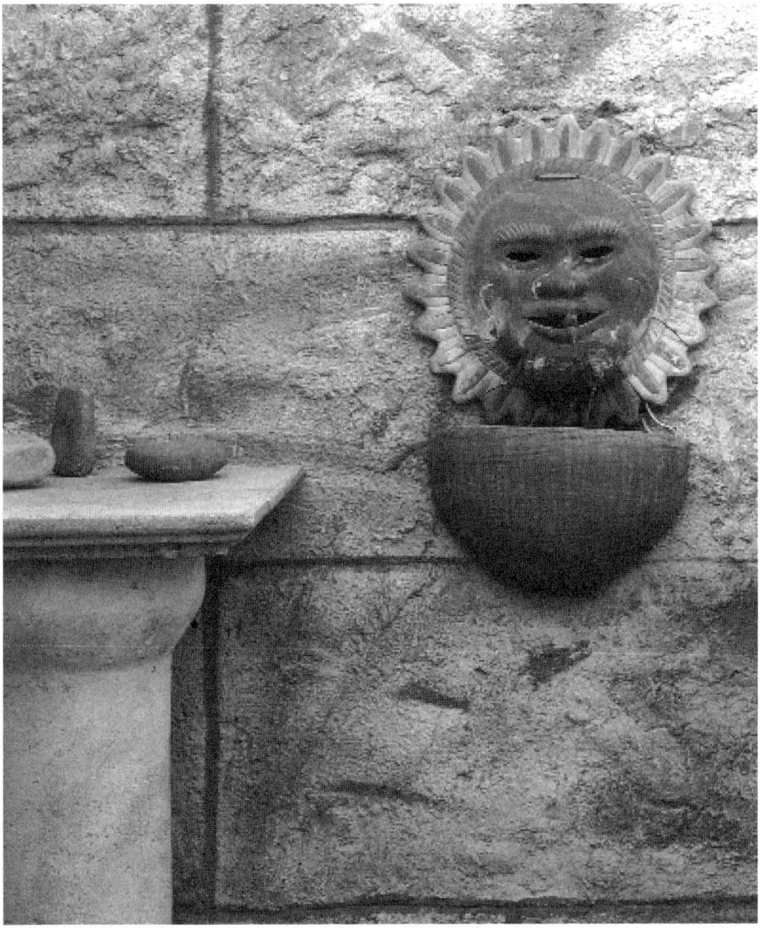

Ravioli Sofia

PASTA:

4 eggs
3 1/2 cups flour, plus more for dusting work surface
1/2 teaspoon olive oil

To make the pasta, make a mound of the flour in the center of a large wooden cutting board or counter. Make a well in the middle of the flour and add the eggs and oil. Using a fork beat together the eggs and oil and begin to incorporate the flour, starting with the inner rim of the well. As you expand the well, keep pushing the flour up to retain the well shape.

Start kneading the dough with both hands, using the palms of your hands. Once you have a smooth mass, remove the dough from the board and scrape up any leftover crusty bits. Discard these bits. Lightly flour the board and continue kneading for 3 more minutes. The dough should be elastic and a little sticky. Continue to knead it for another 3 minutes, remembering to dust your board when necessary. Wrap the dough in plastic and allow it to rest for 30 minutes at room temperature.

Roll out pasta to the second or thinnest setting (depends on personal taste) on a pasta rolling machine and place on a lightly floured surface. Place a teaspoon of the mixture on the dough 1 inch apart on half of the dough. Brush water around the mounds and fold over. It is important to squeeze the mounds with your fist as you must make them air tight. Do not forget to brush water around the mixture as this will help the ravioli stay together. Repeat until all ingredients have been used. Cut out squares and do not worry about straight line cutting. They are truly handmade. These can easily be frozen. Place them on a tray with floured parchment paper in a freezer and when frozen, store them in a container.

To cook- Bring water to boil, add salt and 2 tablespoon olive oil. Boil for 6 to 8 minutes according to taste. (Should be cooked al dente.)

FILLING

20 dried porcini mushrooms
10 sun dried tomatoes (not in oil)
1/2 red onion, chopped
50g (2 oz.) gorgonzola
1 cup Chianti

Soak mushrooms and tomatoes separately in water. (About 2 hours) Drain and squeeze hard so they seem dry. Chop them up. Sauté red onions in skillet with olive oil, then add mushrooms and tomatoes. Toss up and add wine. When the wine has evaporated, remove the skillet from the stove and stir in gorgonzola cheese. Taste and adjust salt. Let cool before putting filling on the pasta.

Serve these with a fresh Marinara sauce.

It is difficult putting this recipe on paper as we don't officially measure. We do it with the eye but readers can always contact us via email for more instructions.

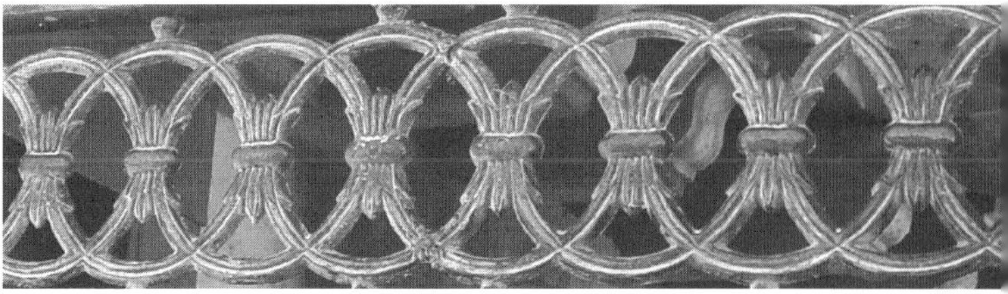

Più su
Renato Zero

E poi
di colpo eccomi qua
sarei arrivato io
in vetta al sogno mio
com'è lontano ieri
e poi
più in alto e ancora su
fino a sfiorare dio
e gli domando io
signore
perché mi trovo qui se non conosco amore
sboccia un fiore malgrado nessuno lo annaffierà
mentre l'aquila fiera in segreto a morire andrà
il poeta si strugge al ricordo di una poesia
questo tempo affamato consuma la mia allegria
canto e piango pensando che un uomo si butta via
che un drogato è soltanto un malato di nostalgia
che una madre si arrende un bambino non nascerà
che potremo restare abbracciati all'eternità
e poi ti ritrovo qui
puntuale al posto tu
tu spettatore vuoi davvero
che io viva il sogno che
non osi vivere te
questa vita ti sfugge se tu non la fermerai
se qualcuno sorride tu non tradirlo mai
la speranza è una musica antica e un motivo in più
canterai e piangerai insieme a me dimmi lo vuoi tu
sveleremo al nemico quel poco di lealtà
insegneremo i perdono a chi dimenticare non sa
la paura che senti è la stessa che provo io
canterai e piangerai insieme a me
fratello mio
più su
più su

più su
ed io mi calerò
nel ruolo che ormai è mio
finché ci crederò
finché ce la farò
più su
più su
più su
fino a sposare il blu
fino a sentire che
ormai sei parte di me
più su
più su

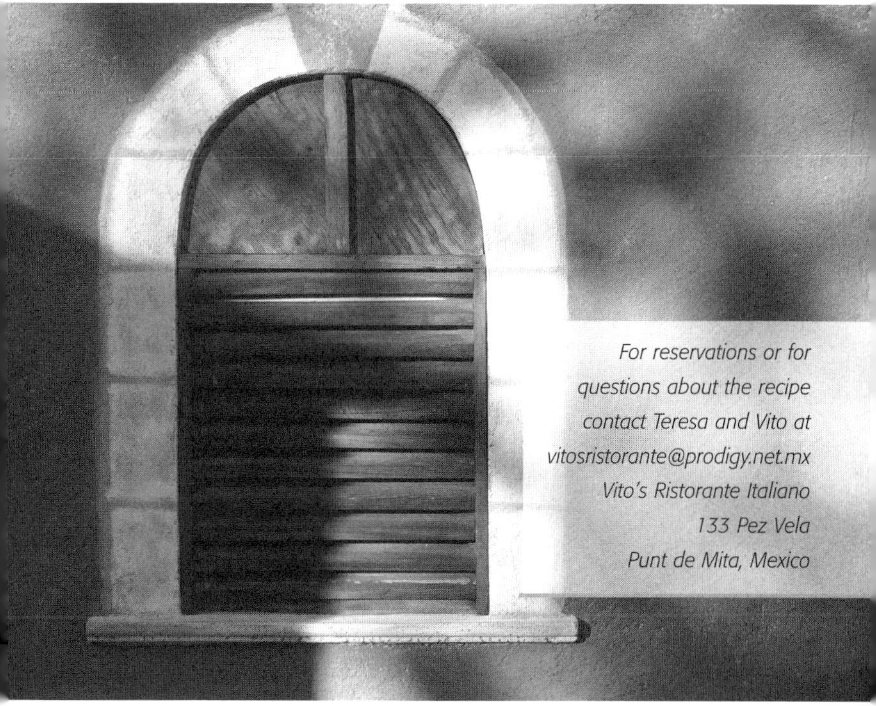

For reservations or for questions about the recipe contact Teresa and Vito at vitosristorante@prodigy.net.mx Vito's Ristorante Italiano 133 Pez Vela Punt de Mita, Mexico

Vicki Reed, Cedarburg, Wisconsin, is a photographer specializing in hand-colored black & white photography. Her work is available at Edgewood Orchard Galleries in Fish Creek, Wisconsin, and on-line at GUILD.com.

Tim Kahl

Poetry (Translation)

Inscricão

By Marly De Oliveira

Eu. E diante da vida,
com meu azul intacto.
Um esbatido de pássaros.
Alto no vento. Grato.

A sensaçao de ser
só, uno, um, completo.
No redondo das horas,
pleno, lúcido, cego.

O que de mim salvando
se vai a cada instante,
nesse morrer diário
e successivo: um canto.

Inscription

Translated by Tim Kahl

Me. In front of life,
with my sky intact.
Birds standing out in relief.
High in the wind. Grateful.

Only the sensation of being,
single, one, complete.
In the round hours,
full, lucid, blind.

What is saving me
runs through every instant,
in this dying diary
and afterwards: a song.

Martírio De Tiradentes

No Cadafalso

Foi um momento de estrelas,
de céu límpido e vazio.
Partiram-se os sete talos
de manhã que alta se abria.
Não houve rios de sangue:
das mãos de Cloto uma dália
serenamente pendia.
E logo, no chão da morte,
os alvos linhos do dia.

The Martyrdom of Tiradentes

At The Gallows

It was a moment of stars,
of the clear and empty sky.
They broke the seven stalks
of morning that opened up heaven.
There will not be rivers of blood:
Cloto's hands
serenely dropped a dahlia.
And then, on death's ground,
the pure lines of the day.

O Esquartejamento

Além da fronteira azul
já se aprimoram os galos,
com fardos de auroras novas
na limpa crista aprumada.
Com exemplo cruel se mostra
o ideal desfeito em nada.

Um fino gume retalha
o muro das enxovias,
e a sombra negra de um pássaro
se acende pelo caminho.
Nenhuma taça se abeira
dos postes a colher vinho.

Vagueira perdida túnica
entre o céu e o chão sem astros.
(Pensar que rosas de música
circundam esferas claras,
quando sobre a terra um corpo
perdeu a harmonia amara!)

The Quartering

Beyond the blue frontier already
the roosters refine themselves,
with the burden of new dawns
at the clean height of their peaks.
With cruel example it shows
the ideal made into nothing.

A fine edge cuts
the walls of the dungeons,
and the black shadow of a bird
is lit up by the road.
No cup draws near the whipping
post to collect wine.

It roamed about in a tunic between
the sky and the starless ground.
(Thinking that the soundhole for
the music is clearly a circle,
when above the earth a body
lost the bitter harmony!)

Reflexão

Sombras de talhe adoçado,
noite no torso da noite.
Não foi nada. Apenas sonho
passado em alvo tamis,
ou rosto só, que da morte
foi bruscamente aprediz.

Mas o mar foi sendo mar,
a terra leito. Houve apenas
entre dois instantes certos
vago tremor de raiz.

Marly de Oliveira was born in Cachoeiro de Itapemerim, Espirito Santo, in 1935. She has lived in Rio de Janeiro, Rome, Buenos Aires, Geneva and Brasilia. She is the author of 14 books of poetry and has translated the works of Jorge Luis Borges and José Guilherme Merquior. She was married to widely-esteemed poet João Cabral Melo Neto, who was thought to be Brazil's leading contender for the Nobel Prize before his death in 1999.

Reflection

Shadows cut sweet,
night in the body of the night.
It was nothing. Barely a dream
passed in white worsted wool,
only the face, that death
was abruptly making into an apprentice.

But the sea was being the sea,
the frame of the earth. Between
two precise moments of time there was
a vague tremor of the hidden cause.

Tim Kahl teaches at Sacramento City College. He has published or has work forthcoming in *Nimrod, American Letters & Commentary, Prairie Schooner, Poetry Motel,* and *Spoon River Poetry Review*, among others. He is currently at work translating German poets Rolf Haufs and Christoph Meckel, and Austrian avant-gardist, Friederike Mayröcker's book of poems/novel, *Das besessene Alter (The Possessed Senior Citizen).*

Charles Nevsimal

Poetry

We Are Different, But We Are One

He tells me
he could never do
what I do.
Could never sit
on barstools night after
night writing poem after
poem, while he is right now
3,200 miles away walking
the Appalachian Trail
from Maine to Carolina
sleeping under stars
counting miles one step
at a time.

He sits around campfires
reading poetry I've sent him
to various mail drops he's
told me about along the way.

Reads them slowly
one by one, then
one by one
he sets them aflame,
my poems
burning beneath the moon
in states I've never been in,
my poems lighting a small section
of wilderness I'll never know.

He tells me my poems, they
light much more than that:
inside, where they stay
despite flame
despite foreign land,
a place where miles can't separate,
a place where he believes
we move to a different beat.

But I assure him, we are one,
and what he doesn't know,
what he couldn't possibly know,
what he might someday learn is
there's a little piece of him
in every poem
he burns.

Charles Nevsimal is from Milwaukee, Wisconsin. Originally from Cedarburg, he writes: "I've been a reader of your publication for some time, now. Thank you for being a beacon of poetry and art in our world. I, too, am a publisher. A few years back, I started Centennial Press. We put out a biannual magazine called *Anthills*, as well as chapbooks and broadsides."

Rosemary M. Magee

Fiction

Spectacular Lies

Each night before she went to sleep, she tasted the stars. Sometimes they were thin and sharp like a Lifesaver that she'd been sucking on; other nights their lustrous insides were round and cold like a sweet drop of white chocolate. Blaise tried to swallow the smaller stars to feel them inside of her, but she could only taste the shape, size, color, and texture as they shifted with the moon over the course of the month. She slept with her blinds open so that her tongue could touch the stars, allowing them to tickle the roof of her mouth in just the way she imagined sparkling champagne might on New Year's Eve.

By day, Blaise avoided her mother, who spent her time answering newspaper ads. Not ads, really– not like "DWF seeks travel companion (M or F but not married)," which were the ones Jesse's mother examined each day. Jesse reported that her mother had made a New Year's resolution to give up drinks after work with married men; they were too tortured. This decision was disappointing to Jesse and Blaise, who liked to spy from the kitchen on the strange males who kissed Jesse's mother in front of the fireplace. Jesse and Blaise invented families for the men. Most of them drove a Camry, which corresponded with a house in the suburbs, they way they figured it. Jesse's mother was now on the lookout for men who owned SUVs. They were more adventuresome types.

But those weren't the kind of ads that Blaise's mother answered. She read the *New York Times Book Review*, where people working on biographies of poets, scientists, and explorers submitted queries. "Anyone with personal anecdotes about Jacques Cousteau, please send them to me for a study I am doing of his life and work." Or, "I am compiling a history of the suffragist movement and would like access to any papers on this subject from the early 20th century." Blaise's mother arranged and re-arranged the clippings like a stack of cards in a never-ending game of solitaire then taped them to the wall in the living room above her computer. There were no sofas or easy chairs in the apartment, just two matching workstations in the living room.

On the first Thursday of the New Year, when Blaise arrived home from school, the latest addition had appeared. Her mother received the *Book Review* early, before Sunday, because she had a subscription just to it. She was not concerned with business, sports, or politics in the other sections. Blaise perused the new clipping. "I want to write the story of Amelia Earhart's final flight. Anyone with any information about the preparations for the flight, please notify me. Thank you very much."

The inquiries were always concise and polite. Blaise reread this one. Her mother watched from the entryway, her amber eyes radiating energy, as if she had just accomplished a feat of enormous consequence. Each week she devised answers to the queries and sent them to the address indicated.

"Why do you suppose anyone would want to write something more about Amelia Earhart? Aren't there enough books about her already?" Blaise scowled in disapproval.

"Because those things are important to do. Just like Sarah Bernhardt and Simone de Beauvoir– the story of all of their lives must be retold, over and over again." Her mother, who tended to be illogical and optimistic, smiled as she spoke. "She was a great person."

"Who?" Blaise had to constantly check on reality, as her mother tended to shift from one topic to the next without notice.

"Why, Amelia, of course." The eyelids closed tightly as if to conceal her inner radiance, then opened wide again. "That's who we're talking about, aren't we?" Her mother added nervously, "Did you mail the letters today?"

Blaise disregarded the question in order to continue the quarrel. "If she was so great, why couldn't you have named me after *her*?" This was a constant controversy between the two of them. Blaise kept a mental list of great people she should have been named after— Marie Curie, for example.

To which her mother responded, "Philosophy is more important than science. Besides, Pascal was both a scientist and a philosopher. A child prodigy, he was."

"Or what about Louisa?"

"Pure sentimental drivel. Anyway, get satisfied with Blaise. It's unique." She paused to ponder her daughter's leftover scowl. "Surely you agree it's better than Ludwig or Wolfgang." That was the way her mother liked to argue– from a position of absurdity. "Don't you think?"

"Emily," Blaise shot back emphatically. She struggled to get the last word in these discussions. "Celeste," she muttered inwardly the name she had secretly given herself.

"'The heart has its reasons..." This familiar refrain steered her mother into the kitchen, where she filled up the tea kettle with water.

Blaise grabbed her backpack and stomped towards her bedroom. She pounced on the bed and searched longingly out the window. The stuffed backpack spilled its contents of books and papers and rumpled, stamped, rectangular envelopes on the floor. It would be hours before the stars arrived. She envied Jesse, who claimed that her mother had chosen an outlaw's name for her. Because she'd been named for a philosopher, Blaise felt pressured to have serious, brilliant thoughts. She'd been told by the gifted and talented teacher that she had a high IQ, so there was no excuse not to reach her full potential. She ought to be able to come up with important ideas to contemplate. But all she could get her mind to focus on was the pair of boots that were on sale at the Rack Room for 25% off. She had hoped against all hope that her father would buy them for her for Christmas, but she only got a card from him. Her mother received a monthly check; Blaise was not allowed to touch it. She wanted to send an inquiry to the *Book Review*, "For a memoir I am writing about my father, please tell him to send me a recent picture. I haven't seen him in a very long time." Would her mother respond with a real picture or some made-up fantasy?

Blaise searched her room for some small token of her father, but his fleeting presence in her life was confirmed by only a few deteriorating photographs. In one, he held her newborn body tight against his wide chest. She tried to decipher his body language, which might provide the key to a secret code. His tight, straight smile signaled unspoken worries while his gray eyes focused on a faraway object. She wanted to remember how massive his hands must have felt as they supported her malleable back and soft infant head. Blaise threw the photograph on the floor with the other papers.

How could he have let her mother give her the name of Blaise anyway? What kind of insensitive beast was he– to name her after a man, a dead, ancient one at that? His other children from his first marriage had sensible, feminine names like Caroline and Anna. She didn't think Louisa would have been such a bad choice. It wasn't drivel to her– those four sisters plotting escapades. Their father was mostly gone also. Plus people always spelled her name wrong– B-L-A-Z-E, like she might be a horse instead of a teenage girl.

Blaise sat up to peer in the mirror above her dresser across the room. She frowned at her reflection, knowing full well she'd never have a boyfriend. Her future prospects were dim, despite the IQ tests. Jesse was in with the group of slow learners, but her destiny unfurled before her like one of the dazzling scarves in her mother's closet. Who'd want to kiss a girl with a name like Blaise and big hips and no boots? Her own mother was utterly useless in terms of planning a reasonable social life. With all of those clippings stuck to the living room wall, it was impossible to invite friends over. Jesse's apartment was more suitable for a happy and fulfilling life.

The ring of the telephone into their normally-hushed apartment startled Blaise. She lifted the receiver just as her mother was responding in a distant but civil tone.

"Yes. How are you doing?"

"I'm calling about Friday night." Jesse's mother spoke

quickly, as if in a panic. "I have some plans." The two mothers rarely talked to one another, except to arrange sleepovers. "Tomorrow, that is."

"I see." These words made Blaise flinch. Her mother never even tried to encourage people to express their feelings.

"It's about the girls." Jesse's mother paused to take a deep breath. "Well, actually, just Jesse, I suppose."

Usually the two girls spent Friday nights at Jesse's place eating pizza and watching horror movies that terrified them.

"I was wondering if they, I mean if she, could stay with you this Friday."

"That would be fine."

"Oh." Jesse's mother clearly expected people to be more talkative. "Are you sure?"

"Yes, of course. We'll expect Jesse for dinner."

Blaise hung up the phone despondently. She sat on the bed, recklessly kicking the loose papers, photograph, and stamped envelopes under her bed with the others. She preferred to spend the whole weekend at Jesse's and to read *Cosmopolitan* beneath the covers, articles about how to have a wild sex life. True, on those nights she missed the stars. Blocked by the window shade in Jesse's room, their secret stories were withheld from her. But she found other pleasures— like listening to the laughter and whispers in the living room. Blaise would close her eyes and imagine touching and tasting the stars as they cascaded through the dense atmosphere of her mind.

Rolling over onto her stomach, Blaise pushed her broad hip bones into the folds of the comforter. She unfastened her jeans, which were too tight, and yawned sadly into her pillow. When would her father rescue her from this dreary life? No wonder he'd left them. A house in the suburbs would be just fine for the two of them, Blaise and her father. Jesse could come to visit, and they'd take long walks in the neighborhood, looking inside people's picture windows to examine how they conducted orderly suburban lives. Her mother wouldn't be bothered by her anymore. And Blaise wouldn't need to worry every day about mailing letters full of invented truths. She'd change her name and get the boots for her birthday, even though it would be summer by then.

After school that Friday, before Jesse's mother came home, the two girls investigated her chest of drawers and tried on her lingerie over their jeans and t-shirts. All the while, Blaise knew that back in her own apartment, just one floor below, her mother was stationed in front of the computer, staring at those inquiries, and writing people she'd never meet about things she knew nothing about. On credit card applications, her mother listed her occupation as "free-lance writer." But responding to random queries was the real way she occupied herself when she could be trying out new things in life, like finding a man. First, however, Blaise knew she'd have to convince her to get a haircut. Her mother's style was very straight and severe around her tight, tired face that used to be pretty, but had given up trying anymore. Blaise believed her mother needed a new outfit, something that would make her feel young and alluring again—like the kind of thing they were trying on right then and there. She twirled a black lace camisole on her index finger. What if she stuffed it in her jeans pocket, later planting it in the dirty clothes basket for her mother to find the next time she did laundry? Just then the two girls heard Jesse's mother open the apartment door. They recklessly tossed the lingerie back into a drawer and ran pell-mell down the hallway towards Jesse's room, where they flung themselves on the bed in a tangle of giggles.

"Do you think this one is short enough?"

Jesse's mother stood up straight, letting her ample chest protrude against the tight knit top. A pile of discarded garments grew around her feet. This was going to be a real date with dinner and dancing, not just drinks at a bar while the girls stayed at Blaise's apartment for the night, according to the terms negotiated by the two mothers.

Jesse nodded, sucking on a strand of blonde curls, while Blaise shook her head decisively no. She thought Jesse's mom should look as sexy as possible. According to *Cosmo*, men liked short dresses, especially if there was dancing involved.

"How 'bout this one?" She selected a black, filmy item from the pile. It had lavish lace on the top.

"That's a slip, honey-bunch." Mrs. Jennings used lots of pet names. She had asked Blaise to call her Wanda since she technically wasn't a "Mrs." anyway. Blaise did not like the name Wanda. It was too homely for Jesse's spirited mother.

"Oh." Blaise tried to recover. "Well, it's pretty enough to be a dress. And nice and short." Mrs. Jennings watched her from behind the closet door where the full-length mirror was hung. "Maybe you could just wear a blouse over it?" Blaise suggested softly, as if to herself.

Jesse laughed with a sneer, spitting out the wet curls. She knew Blaise had no experience in these things. Her mother turned to give her a dirty look, then fixed her attention on Blaise, whose neck was starting to feel prickly-hot with the three of them all crammed in the bedroom together.

"You know something? That's not such a bad idea." Mrs. Jennings eyed the black item under discussion.

"It would be real sexy," reasoned Blaise. "Like this one in *Cosmo*." The picture showed a woman lounging on a sofa with just a slip and pantyhose. Her lips and legs were parted seductively.

Mrs. Jennings pulled her dress over her head and tossed it on the bed. She wore skimpy underwear that revealed parts of her body that Blaise did not recall ever seeing on her own mother. She sucked in her protruding stomach. Mrs. Jennings reached for the slip and stepped into it.

"Like this?"

She turned a full circle. Her hips were nice and slim. Blaise wanted to look just like her, the way Jesse was starting to shape up. The slip clung ever so slightly to the rounded parts of her.

"Yes, you look very, very sexy," Blaise asserted. Jesse snickered again, but now Blaise knew that she'd found the right solution for Mrs. Jennings. "Just put on black hose, and you'll be perfect."

Lately that was all Blaise could think about– how some people looked sexy and others didn't. She knew what category she and her mother fit into. They were condemned to a life of cotton underwear. Her father must have figured out their fate as well, which was why he had decided to escape. Maybe he would like Jesse's mother. The four of them could all live in the suburbs together.

"Then that's what I'll wear. You have great taste, sugar." She walked over to Blaise and pulled back her stringy, beige hair into a ponytail. "And beguiling amber eyes, you know." Blaise turned away, embarrassed. Slippery perspiration beads squiggled down her forehead. She peered into the mirror across the room. Fatigued eyes were reflected back to her– just the way her mother's looked. She'd been trying to stay awake at night to observe the movement of the stars in order to plot their paths. She now imagined dancing elegantly with them against the black-velvet sky trimmed with lace.

"So, what are you two girls up to tonight?"

Blaise did not like it when her mother tried to manufacture conversations. It was awkward and embarrassing, plus there was the worrisome matter of the unmailed letters.

"We'll just watch TV in my bedroom," she replied in a terse monotone.

Her mother did not approve of television, but she usually allowed Blaise do what she wanted to do, especially when Jesse was over.

"How 'bout some dinner, Jesse?"

"No thank you, Mrs. Terrell. My mother got us some roast beef sandwiches from Arby's. We already ate."

Blaise's mother looked annoyed.

"They were five for five dollars. We had a coupon," explained Jesse. She and her mother were always bargain hunting. Blaise knew this would not impress her own mother, who often served up fruit and cheese and apple juice to guests, while she drank tea in carefully-calculated sips.

Blaise worried that Jesse would no longer like her when they got older. Everything about her life seemed tarnished and lopsided while Jesse spun around her in bright circles. Still, Jesse saved her a seat in the school cafeteria at lunchtime. She tried hard to participate in the conversations with the other girls, which was why she stayed current on all the *Cosmopolitan* issues. It put her ahead of those who only read *Seventeen*.

"Hey, Jess. Let's go." She needed to direct Jesse away from her mother so that she wouldn't see their life up close. "It's time to watch *Seinfeld*." The two girls abandoned Blaise's mother, staring at the computer screen. She kept all of the lights on in the living room so that it was as bright as a spaceship. Blaise liked the way Mrs. Jennings lit only a few mood lamps. By contrast, the two computers were brilliantly hygienic. No wonder she and her mother had gray complexions, washed out like the black-and-white photographs in old *Life* magazines.

Blaise purposefully kept her room messy as it was her impression from reading Ann Landers that teenagers were supposed to do that. Jesse reviewed the squalor with admiration. She vaulted on the double bed amid an assortment of battered stuffed animals, found the clicker, and turned on the TV. An over-eager laugh track exploded in the empty space between them. Blaise kicked her entire backpack under the bed.

"Doesn't your mother ever do anything but sit in front of that computer?" Jesse mashed the mute button.

"Sure she does," defended Blaise. "It's just that... well, when we're around that's what she does... you see... so she won't be a bother to us." She didn't like other people analyzing her mother's habits. She needed to reassure Jesse that everything was perfectly normal in their home.

"Like what else?" persisted Jesse.

"Lots of things. All of the things that most people do. In addition to being a writer, she's an artist, you know." Blaise fervently hoped that identifying her mother as an artist would excuse her peculiar behavior.

Jesse did not seem impressed with art. "Doesn't she ever have sex?"

Blaise lay down suddenly and covered her face with a pillow. They often speculated on Jesse's mother's sex life, but they'd never discussed her own mother's private behavior.

"Well, you know, not since my father." Her muffled voice sounded distant, even to herself.

"He's been gone for years." Jesse argued.

"Sometimes they meet to discuss me," Blaise countered. She threw the pillow to the floor.

"And have sex?" Jesse was incredulous. "Where do they meet?"

"Oh." Blaise bit her lip hard. "I... I never get to go. My mother doesn't want me to see him." The metallic taste of blood coated her tongue.

"Maybe she just hates all men."

"Yeah, right. Then why would she name me Blaise? Pascal was a man, you know." She blotted her upper lip with the sheet; a tiny streak of blood emerged.

"Whatever." Jesse turned up the volume. They obsessively watched *Seinfeld* reruns, memorizing the dialogue.

Blaise only half-listened. She propped up her head on the pillow and gazed out the window. There were no stars out yet. Often they waited until late at night– as if to offer her dessert at the end of a dreary day.

"Put down the blinds, will you?" Jesse did not like blank windows. "It's cold in here."

Blaise sat up and tossed her a crocheted comforter. Her grandmother, her father's mother, had made it for her when she was a baby. But she was dead now.

"Use this."

"It's itchy. Plus, you know I don't like it when you leave the blinds open." Jesse was starting to shake. She sucked noisily on the ends of her hair. Every now and then Blaise had an inkling that Jesse didn't know absolutely everything about life. "People will watch us."

"Don't be ridiculous. Anyway, I have to."

"Why?" Jesse's voice had turned inward– like that of a tired toddler.

"It's just the rule in my room."

Jesse shifted over on her side, away from Blaise and away from the window. The two girls were still fully dressed. They did not like to change their clothes in front of one another.

Now Blaise could see some stars. They were shy, so she had to wait patiently for them to appear one by one. She made up stories about them, about the one she called Celeste, creating secret tales of romance– about how they mated with one another and stayed together for life just like certain species of birds and apes. She'd been studying evolution in science, and she'd concluded that stars were more highly evolved than humans. In her mind, on this night, they accompanied Mrs. Jennings while she danced in a sexy slip on her date.

The bed was starting to tremble. Jesse had been so quiet that Blaise assumed she was asleep. But now, faint kitten sounds escaped her. Blaise lay perfectly still. She didn't want to know what Jesse was thinking about. It felt scary to imagine Jesse or her mother ever being sad and lonely. They had everything– pretty clothes from discount warehouses, sexy bodies, admiring looks from men. They had each other while Blaise was all by herself, except for the stars. She would not let Jesse distract her from this time of evening intimacy with them.

Soon the trembling stopped and Jesse breathed heavily

through sniffles. It was safe to assume that she was asleep. When all alone, Blaise sang to the stars. She didn't know much rock music– besides, it was too noisy. The stars wouldn't dance to it. She half-sang and half-hummed the love song from "The Music Man" video that she had watched over and over again. "Goodnight my someone, goodnight my love. Sweet dreams, my someone, sweet dreams, my love." She envisioned her voice traveling to the stars and then bouncing back to earth into her father's house so that he could hear her clear, silver voice.

Jesse moaned and stirred restlessly beside her.

"I have to pee." She grabbed her bag of clothes as she proceeded out the bedroom door. Blaise knew Jesse would change in the bathroom. She turned off the TV so that the room would be nice and dark. She would go to sleep in her clothes. Sticking out her tongue, she tasted the sharp, bright sugar crystals on the points of the stars.

When Blaise woke up, her room was dark and chilly. She reached across the bed to touch Jesse's warmth, but no curled body rested nearby, just the old comforter in an abandoned heap. Blaise sat up with alarm. What had happened to Jesse? Had she returned from the bathroom? The luminous numbers on her clock radio read 12:05 a.m. She longed to drift back to the safety of sleep. The stars were still in the sky. But now her insides were all woozy, the way she imagined Mrs. Jennings felt when she went dancing and had too much to drink. She glanced once more at the stars, grabbed the blanket, and managed to propel herself out of the bedroom.

From the hallway, Blaise could see all the lights on in the living room. Her mother often stayed up the entire night. Usually there was just the clicking of the keyboard at a steady, hasty pace; tonight voices dominated the normally quiet spaces.

She peered into the kitchen. At the scratched oak table sat Jesse with her mother. They were drinking hot tea. The kettle rattled on the stove top. Blaise felt sick to her stomach. When she was not around, her mother was likely to say the most outrageous things. Blaise pulled the comforter around her shoulders.

"I don't know if I will get it, though," Jesse speculated in tearful tones. She gently tugged a slick, dark-blonde curl out of her mouth and inspected it. Blaise's mother nodded sympathetically. "You have to pay extra just to tryout. Then there's the cheerleading uniforms. They don't ever put those on sale." Her voice faltered as her hair collapsed around her distressed face.

"You'd be a splendid cheerleader." Blaise was shocked her mother even acknowledged the existence of cheerleading in the world. She listened with concern.

"Are you feeling better now?"

Jesse nodded demurely. She wore a faded flannel nightgown. Her socks had holes in the toes. She seemed to have shrunk in size since earlier in the day.

"Didn't your mother tell you about all of this?" The amber eyes blinked rapidly with worry.

"Not really, not much anyway. We just learned about it in health last year." Jesse crossed her arms over her abdomen and moved her head in slow motion while she inspected each object in the kitchen as if it were a treasure. Blaise watched her take in everything. Stacks of books threatened to tumble over. Freshly-stuffed, neatly-addressed envelopes stacked on the counter awaited some otherworldly destination. Finally, Jesse's eyes registered the presence of Blaise in the hallway. Blaise's mother shifted in her seat to look. They both then stared at their tea mugs, as if they had been caught in the middle of a midnight conspiracy.

"Hey," Blaise uttered foolishly. The blanket slipped from her shoulders to the floor. Despite her wrinkled jeans and sweatshirt, she felt naked and cold all over.

"Want some hot tea?" her mother inquired. When Blaise had been small, she and her mother had tea parties at all times of the day and night. Lately she'd decided that she hated tea.

Blaise did not respond. Reestablishing the blanket over her shoulders, she took a seat at the table. Before her sat a large, pale-blue box. She shuddered. Sanitary napkins. Things like this were not supposed to happen out in the open. Last summer, she had stared out the window in stony silence when her mother tried to explain it all to her.

Her mother poured spicy, aromatic tea into a mug and handed it to Blaise. The steam hung in the air between them. She then silently excused herself from the table and moved instinctively towards the living room where her computer flickered. Exiting the kitchen, she paused to massage Blaise's shoulders and pat Jesse's head. A minute later, the customary clicking resumed. Blaise and Jesse drank their tea in silence.

The next morning at breakfast, the sanitary napkin box had disappeared. Jesse complained of cramps. Blaise did not respond. How was it possible that this beautiful girl could invade her home, have her period before Blaise had even had one, get up and talk with her mother in the middle of the night, then complain of cramps the next morning? Blaise ate her cereal and noted that the pile of letters now had stamps on them.

"I think I'm going to check on my mother to see if she's home." Jesse's eyes were streaked with red lines.

"Better not go up there yet," Blaise warned. Sometimes the date was still in the apartment. Mrs. Jennings usually was tired and cross when she got up– and not particularly sexy. Jesse looked like she might cry.

"Let's look out the window. Maybe," Blaise suggested hopefully, "there's a car that we don't recognize." They liked to be spies together. Jesse did not seem to mind unadorned windows during the daytime.

In the living room the lights were on, but the computer was off. Blaise's mother often slept through the mornings.

The two girls rubbed their foreheads against the cold

window. Wintry winds blew torn Styrofoam cups into the street. No new cars were parked there.

"You know, your mother is pretty nice." Jesse rubbed her abdomen in gentle circles.

"Is that so?" Blaise replied noncommittally, desperately hoping that a car, any style or model, would materialize to capture their joint attention.

"Yeah, we talked for a long time last night."

"What did you talk about?" This conversation made Blaise nervous, but she couldn't help pursuing it.

"All of those clippings."

Blaise swallowed hard. "What about the clippings?" she whispered.

"I asked her why she did that. What she did with them."

"Hmm. Really." Blaise had never had the courage to ask her mother that question directly. She resented Jesse's open curiosity. "What did she say?"

"At first she just said, 'the heart has its reasons...'"

Blaise groaned. Her own stomach was starting to tighten up in cramps. She tried to picture sexy Mrs. Jennings in that silky black slip with a man's arms wrapped around her, his breath hot like smoke in her ear.

Jesse maintained her focus. "But then she said something about, well, something about she was doing it for you." She paused as if trying to capture a thought that had escaped. "So that you could learn about their spectacular lives."

"For *me*?" Blaise was shocked. She never thought of her mother as doing anything for her. "Don't believe it. It's only for herself, not for anyone else."

"Well, that's what she told me, and I *do* believe her. We looked at the ones about Amelia Earhart and Emily Dickinson and Juliette Gordon Lowe. She said that they were all elec–electric. Or something like that– one of those vocabulary words."

"Eccentric."

"Yep, that's it."

"Well, so what?"

"That's what girls have to be, she said. Ec–eccentric."

"She oughta know." Blaise remained unimpressed. But the image of her mother talking about cheerleading and telling Jesse stories over tea made her feel utterly forsaken. Besides, Jesse did not know the whole truth– about how her mother answered these requests for information with made-up stories. How could you ever explain anything like that? It was spectacular *lies*, not lives. Blaise's sore lip throbbed with the thought of that kind of nearby eccentricity. She bumped her head hard against the windowsill in order to feel the painfulness of reality. Jesse was watching her. It was time to change the subject.

"Anyway, maybe we should check on your mother." The street below was coming alive, and the rest of the world was moving beyond them. "I don't see any SUVs."

Jesse did not respond. She fingered a new, dry curl, clenching it between her large front teeth with enormous concentration. Their faces had created a steamy smudge on the windowpane.

"I bet my dad has a new SUV by now." Blaise spoke with superior confidence, as if he might rescue her at any moment from the edge of the cold abyss.

Jesse released the curl as she emitted a high, disgusted laugh. "Why don't you just give up on him? He's never coming back to you."

Blaise would not let Jesse, whose father was in prison for forgery, upset her today. No wonder she had given up; he was a criminal. But Blaise's father was a lawyer who prosecuted criminals. The two had absolutely nothing in common. Blaise pressed her shoulder against the window, blocking Jesse's view.

"It's like this," she explained deliberately, the way her math teacher taught fractions to the slow students. She'd thought this issue through many times but had never told anyone except the stars. "If he doesn't return, then... then I've lost nothing by believing he would. If he does come back, I'll feel happy– you know, satisfied– that he and I, well, that I never let him go."

Jesse collected all of her curls into one enormous, blonde bouquet and wrapped them around her pale, pink hand. She stretched her neck to look past Blaise towards the empty street below. Their shoulders touched, pulled apart, hesitated, and then touched again. A merged shadow, cast on the living room wall, hovered protectively behind them.

"Well, let's go upstairs. We need to make sure my mother's okay," Jesse suggested in a new quiet voice.

Blaise nodded in acquiescence. "I wonder if the outfit worked." She felt responsible for how things had gone the night before.

As the two girls left the living room, Blaise switched off the lights. The smell of sweet, spiced tea lingered in the air. She reached into the kitchen to collect the letters and stashed them in her back pocket. Maybe she'd mail them this time after all– so that her mother could keep on believing whatever it was she needed to believe. Blaise grabbed her jacket from the hall rack and turned to survey the familiar surroundings. The blank computer screen emitted deep, empty knowledge into the living room. When she came back, everything would be turned on again, predictable and bright just like the stars she loved. All day long, she hoarded their penetrating light inside of her until at night, once again, they appeared in the lavish sky to dance across silky black infinity.

Rosemary M. Magee is Senior Associate Dean at Emory University and Executive Director of the Arts Project. Her writing– which includes literary essays as well as fiction– has been published in a wide range of journals and magazines, including *Fine Print, Iron Horse Literary Review, Atlanta Magazine,* and *Sanskrit.* A regular artist-in-residence at the Hambidge Center in North Georgia, she is working on a collection of short stories. She lives with her husband and children in Decatur, Georgia.

Stephen Massimilla

Poetry

Time

In the dream of the absolute
to which

to fall,
I believe

you smiled with your eyes
shut.

Fury of night, throw
the big thing out there, a revelation...

There
can be none.

All my life I misunderstood
pain, wandered in a maze

of urban noise.
Never touched an ocean.

Almost Past That

1.
By dusk the lake was
not there, the bed looking
as it hadn't. I sensed a question

in your eyes (of a luster
often seen on tea pots,
rarely on people), or maybe

you had nothing left to ask.
You were not you at all,
I thought, as shadows

migrated through leaves
and hung in the branches.
Last night I was never

in my life a child.
The day to come was a myth.
There was nowhere else.

2.
This morning, leaves shake
at the dim-lit glass, faint paisley
of autumn on the back

of everything. Suddenly
last night seems like
illusion, outlived by a wish, also

innocent until I called
it this, which looks back
for the hint of a kettle's breath,

to where I like to think, I thought,
I like to know the faintest things.
I know enough to know

most things worth knowing
are past that, you and I, and should
withdraw from all we half-

know, but reach instead
right towards you, limp in sleep,
and touch your head.

Stephen Massimilla is a poet and visual artist from Sea Cliff, New York. His book *Forty Floors From Yesterday* (Bordighera Press) received the Sonia Raiziss-Giop Series Bordighera Poetry Prize. Massimilla's poems have appeared in *Tampa Review, Epoch, Puerto del Sol, The High Plains Literary Review*, and many other journals and anthologies.

Submission Guidelines

Porcupine is published twice each year. Issues contain a mixture of poetry, short fiction, essays, feature interviews, and visual art work. Cover art is occasionally selected from submitted material. We welcome unsolicited manuscripts and art work throughout the year. There are no restrictions as to theme or style. Prose should be readable, professional, and of a high quality. Make us care about the characters. Poetry should be accessible and highly selective. If a submission is not timely for one issue, it will be considered for another.

Send a sampling of visual art work, one prose piece, or one to three poems at a time (mail genres separately). Art work should be submitted as transparencies or digital files. We can accommodate a limited number of full color reproductions. Black and white is encouraged. Prose should be double spaced on one side only and should be no longer than twenty-five pages (shorter pieces will receive stronger consideration). Although we are interested primarily in short stories, novel excerpts are acceptable if self-contained. Poems should be individually typed on one side of the page. Each page should include the author's name. Feature interviews are commissioned and are not accepted without prior arrangement. Previously published material or simultaneous submissions are not considered.

It is recommended that the magazine be reviewed prior to submitting material (send $5.00 for a sample copy). Manuscripts should be submitted as imbedded email text (ppine259@aol.com) or mailed with SASE to: Porcupine, PO Box 259, Cedarburg, WI 53012. The outside of the envelope should state: "Fiction," "Essay," "Poetry," or "Art Work." Unsolicited material sent directly to an editor's home or office will be discarded. Expect ten to twelve weeks for a response. Payment is one copy upon publication.

Back Issues Available
$5.00 including shipping within USA

Volume 1 Issue 1

Cover Art: Polly Ewens
Interviews: *Peggy Hong* by Amy Franklin, *Thomas Kubala* by Howard Hinterthuer, *Guillermo Menocal* by Jeanette Hurt
Essay: Barbara Joosse
Fiction: Carol Lynn Schowalter, Christine Tachick
Poetry: Judith M. Ford, Hilary Goldblatt, Greg Grummer, Thea Kovac, Julie Parson-Nesbitt, Kenneth Pobo, W.A. Reed, Robert Siegel, Debra Kay Vest
Portfolio: Photographs of Maine by Vicki Reed
Visual Arts: Sally Duback, Doug Edmunds, Polly Ewens, Thomas Kubala, Sarah McEneany, Carri M. Skoczek, Vicki Reed

Volume 1 Issue 2

Cover Art: Vicki Reed and Robert Reddy
Interviews: *Thomas Hoffman* by Mona Bernstein, *Tony Finlayson* by Peggy Hong, *Martin Jack Rosenblum* by W.A. Reed
Fiction: Mary Ann Cain, Dennis Must, Philip Russel
Poetry: Amy E. De Jarlais, Susan Firer, Kimiko Hahn, Kristin Herbert, Karen Haas-Howland, Thor Ringler, Joseph Rubano, Cheryl Whitehead
Portfolio: Photographs by Doug Edmunds
Visual Arts: Mona Bernstein, Doug Edmunds, Susan Falkman, Thomas Hoffman, Leo Pilak, Vicki Reed

Volume 2 Issue 1

Cover Art: *Five Red Horses With Lilies* by Katye Rueth
Interviews: *Jean Crane* by Loretta Strehlow, *Brana Kevich* by Barbara Joosse, *Charles Radtke* by W.A. Reed
Fiction: Thomas David Lisk, Matthew Roberson, J.L. Schneider, Carol Lynn Schowalter
Poetry: Jacqueline Berger, Ann Hostetler, Martha Kranzthor-Osvat, E.O. Lipchik, Helen Robertson, Loretta Strehlow, T.N. Turner
Portfolio: Paintings by Katye Rueth
Visual Arts: Jean Crane, Doug Edmunds, Brana Kevich, Charles Radtke, Vicki Reed, Katye Rueth

Johnson Heritage Post

115 W. WISCONSIN ST., P.O. BOX 35
GRAND MARAIS, MN 55604-9663
(218) 387-2314
ON THE HARBOR IN DOWNTOWN GRAND MARAIS

Customer's Order No. Date

Name: Mrs. Cyd

Address: Knife River, Mn

SOLD BY	CASH	C.O.D.	CHARGE	ON ACCT.	

QTY.	DESCRIPTION	AMOUNT
1	Porcupine Map w/ tax	9.62
		9.67

ALL claims and returned goods MUST be accompanied by this bill.

Volume 2 Issue 2

Cover Art: David Lenz

Interviews: *David Lenz* by W.A Reed,
R.J.Siegel by Howard Hinterthuer,
Teri Wagner by Karen Haas-Howland

Fiction: Melodie Starkey

Poetry: Susanne R. Bowers, Bill Embly, Leon De Greiff/(Guevara),
John Grey, Elizabeth Ann James,
B.Z. Niditch, Ilana Simons

Portfolio: Sculpture by Truman Lowe

Visual Arts: Doug Edmunds, David Lenz, Truman Lowe,
Vicki Reed, Teri Wagner

Volume 3 Issue 1 (Sold Out)

Cover Art: *Goat Boys* by Betty LaDuke

Interviews: *Mireille Favarel* by Mark Cebulski,
Betty LaDuke by Barbara Joosse,
Stanislav Venglevski by W.A. Reed

Fiction: Karen Sharp, Martha Highers

Poetry: Holly Day, Barbara DeCesare, Christine Delea,
Paul J. Enea, Sarah Fox, Andrew Genn-Dorian,
John Grey, B.Z. Niditch, Simon Perchik, Kenneth Pobo,
G.K. Wuori

Portfolio: Photographs of Africa by Vicki Reed

Visual Arts: Betty LaDuke, Vicki Reed

Volume 3 Issue 2

Cover Art: *Lily and Sunflower*, Polaroid transfers by
Sarah McEneany

Interviews: *Joel Pfeiffer* by Barbara Joosse,
Jon Van Zyle by Howard Hinterthuer

Fiction: Paul Lewellan, Terri Brown-Davidson, C.J. Muchhala, Ian
MacMillan, Lydia Webster

Poetry: Arlene Ang, Taylor Graham, Meghan Hickey,
Katherine Holmes, Joan Payne Kincaid, B.Z. Niditch,
Jim Redmond, Todd Evan Temkin, Laurie Ann Whitt

Portfolio: Photographs by Sarah McEneany

Visual Arts: Doug Edmunds, Joel Pfeiffer,
Sarah McEneany, Jon Van Zyle

Volume 4 Issue 1

Cover Art: Ladislav Hanka
Interviews: *Ladislav Hanka* by Barbara Joosse, *Orunamamu* by Howard Hinterthuer, *Evelyn Patricia Terry* by W.A. Reed
Fiction: Teri Brown Davidson, Mary Ann Cain, Laura Davis, Tex Kerschen
Poetry: James Armstrong, Tom Baer, Mike Catalano, M.C. Cheung, Daniel Corrie, Richard Fein, Alan Harawitz, Ward Kelley, Janet McCann, Abby Millager, C J Muchhala, Tina Twito, Ryan G. Van Cleave
Portfolio: Jewelry by Elaine Unzicker
Visual Arts: Doug Edmunds, Ladislav Hanka, Vicki Reed, Evelyn Patricia Terry, Elaine Unzicker

Volume 4 Issue 2 (Sold Out)

Cover Art: Jin Xu
Interviews: *Anne Irene Haberland* by Barbara Joosse, *Bob Reddy* by W.A. Reed
Essay: Stephen Cucé
Fiction: Jeanne Farewell, Karl Voskuil, Rob Yardumian
Poetry: Barry Ballard, Loren Baum, Susanne Bowers, Judith Ford, James Grabill, Jessica Hank, Dan Hintz, Martin Hintz, Gillian Kiley, Joan Payne Kincaid, Pat Ranzoni, Stefan Sencerz, Virgil Suárez, Peter Tomassi, Jane Varley, Phyllis Wax, Frederick Zydek,
Portfolio: Sculpture and Painting by Jin Xu
Visual Arts: Doug Edmunds, Anne Irene Haberland, Bob Reddy, Vicki Reed, Jin Xu

Volume 5 Issue 1

Cover Art: Schomer Lichtner
Interviews: *Schomer Lichtner* by Barb Joosse *Chris Thomson* by Charley Radtke
Fiction: Holly Day, Yang Huang, Nicole Moss
Poetry: Judith Barisonzi, Larsen Bowker, Catherine Daly, Fliss, Taylor Graham, John Grey, Robert Grunst, Daniel Hansen, Taj Jackson, Joanne Lowery, B.Z. Niditch, Douglas O'Connor, Erica Olsen, Simon Perchik, Kenneth Pobo, Elisha Porat, Virgil Suárez, Rodney Torreson, Ellen Wernecke
Portfolio: Paintings by Ruth Grotenrath
Visual Arts: Sarah McEneany, Schomer Lichtner

Volume 5 Issue 2 (Sold Out)

Cover Art: Santiago Calatrava
Interviews: *Tom Uttech* by Barb Joosse
Dale Chihuly by W.A. Reed
Fiction/Essay: Anne Benson, Beth Bretl, Michelle DuVal, Judith M. Ford, Jeffrey Perso, Pamela Reitman
Poetry: Gale Acuff, William Aiken, Richard Alan Bunch, Catherine Carter, Carol Frith, Nilay Gandhi, Ward Kelley, Thomas David Lisk, Ron Mohring, Robert Nazarene, Eve Rifkah, Catherine Sexton, Virgil Suárez, T.N. Turner, Ryan G. Van Cleave, Anca Vlasopolos, George Wallace
Portfolio: Architecture by Santiago Calatrava
Visual Arts: Dale Chihuly, Sarah McEneany, Vicki Reed, Tom Uttech

Volume 6 Issue 1

Cover Art: Christopher Copeland
Interviews: *Flora Langlois* by Barb Joosse
Luoyong Wang by W.A. Reed
Fiction/Essay: Meghan Hickey, Mark Krueger, Virgil Suárez, William Woods
Poetry: Antler, Barry Ballard, Terri Brown-Davidson, Jennifer Dick, Kathryn Gahl, Zan Gay, Jeremy James George, Taylor Graham, John Grey, Carol Hamilton, Meghan Hickey, Joan Payne Kincaid, David Lawrence, Thomas David Lisk, A. Loudermilk, Charlotte McCaffrey, Robin Merigan, Ben Miller, CJ Muchhala, Linden Ontjes, John Parras, Kenneth Pobo, Jim Redmond, Stephen R. Roberts, Anne Silver, George Staehle, Lydia Webster, Anne Pierson Wiese
Portfolio: Christopher Copeland
Visual Arts: Flora Langlois, JoAnne Russo

Volume 6 Issue 2

Cover Art: Dennis Nechvatal
Interview: *John Horváth, Jr.* by Ward Kelley
Stage Play: Tom Patrick
Fiction/Essay: Jessica Gunderson, Sandra Hunter, Kathe Lison, Lisa Summers
Poetry: Guy R. Beining, Michael Broek, R.S. Carlson, David Cazden, Dane Cervine, Robert Cooperman, Eva Alice Counsell, Carol Hamilton, Nancy A. Henry, Rebecca Helen Galloway, James B. Livingston, Duane Locke, Jessica Martin, Susan Maurer, James Norcliffe, Jack Rickard, Virginia Schnurr, Elizabeth S. Volpe
Portfolio: Dennis Nechvatal
Visual Arts: Dennis Nechvatal

Volume 7 Issue 1

Cover Art: Bill Meyer
Fiction/Essay: David Bulley, Terrence J. Coffman, Kathryn Gahl, Morton Inger, Ward Kelley, Michael Kula
Poetry: Antler, Arlene Ang, Barry Ballard, B.J. Best, Anupama Bhargava, Richard Alan Bunch, Suzanne Burns, Nick Foster, James Grabill, Ward Kelley, Prasenjit Maiti, Angela Menking, Joddy Murray, S.M. Page, Michael D. Roberts, Marina Rubin, Paul Sohar/ Sándor Kányádi, Doug Tanoury, Jillian Weise
Portfolio: Vicki Reed
Visual Arts: Bill Meyer

Volume 7 Issue 2

Cover Art: Vicki Reed
Interviews: *Antler* by Brandon Lewis
Terese Agnew by Glenn Adamson
Fiction/Essay: Laurie Arendt, Colin Garrett, Ann Minoff, W.A. Reed Andrew Zornoza
Poetry: Ace Boggess, Antler, Chris Crittenden, David Dooley, Susan Hazen-Hammond, Dale M. Kushner, Brandon Lewis, Paul D. McGlynn, Robin Merrill, Vladimir Orlov, Daniel Polikoff/Rainer Maria Rilke, Virgil Suárez, Ian Woollen
Portfolio: Threaded Metaphors: Text & Textiles
Visual Arts: Terese Agnew

To Order Single Issues or Subscriptions

Return this form with a check or money order to:
Porcupine, P.O. Box 259, Cedarburg, WI 53012

Name ______________________________
(please print)

Street Address ______________________________

City, State, Zip ______________________________

Yes, I'm subscribing to Porcupine:
☐ One Year ($15.95 for two Issues)
☐ Two Years ($30.95 for four Issues)
Begin my subscription with: Volume____ Issue____

Enter a gift subscription for:

Name ______________________________
(please print)

Street Address ______________________________

City, State, Zip ______________________________

☐ One Year ($15.95 for two Issues)
☐ Two Years ($30.95 for four Issues)
Begin my subscription with: Volume____ Issue____

Sign gift card: ______________________________
(Write additional gift subscriptions on a separate piece of paper)

I wish to order the following single copies:

_Vol. 1, Issue 1	_Vol. 2, Issue 1	N/A Vol. 3, Issue 1	_Vol. 4, Issue 1
_Vol. 1, Issue 2	_Vol. 2, Issue 2	_Vol. 3, Issue 2	N/A Vol. 4, Issue 2
_Vol. 5, Issue 1	_Vol. 6, Issue 1	_Vol. 7, Issue 1	_Vol. 8, Issue 1
N/A Vol. 5, Issue 2	_Vol. 6, Issue 2	_Vol. 7, Issue 2	

Number of single copies ordered ____ x $5.00 = ________

Number of One Year Subscriptions ____ x $15.95 = ________

Number of Two Year Subscriptions ____ x $30.95 = ________

Total Amount Enclosed ________

We Support *the* Arts...

Because each artist works to share with us
a spark of creativity that just might ignite
our own dreams.

Reddy & Associates

Graphic design services for businesses and institutions–giving form to insights.

P.O. Box 639, Cedarburg, WI 53012
(262) 377-8448

U-Line Corporation

Pioneers in Refrigeration

8900 N.55th St., Milwaukee, WI 53223

(414) 354-0300 Email: u-line@execpc.com
Web Site: www.u-line.com

Washington House Inn

A country Victorian inn located in the heart of Cedarburg.

W62 N573 Washington Avenue, Cedarburg, WI 53012
(262) 375-3550 Outside Wisconsin: (800) 554-4717

Gift Certificates available
Web Site: www.washingtonhouseinn.com